**Coach Your Team**

Liz Hall is an award-winning and internationally re-nowned accredited coach and journalist, and a trained mindfulness teacher based in Spain and the UK. She has worked with a range of clients from organizations including Green Alliance, KPMG, CIPD, the NHS, News UK, Portsmouth University and Reed Business Information. She is an expert on mindful coaching and regularly runs mindful coaching workshops in the UK and internationally. She has written for publications including the *Guardian*, the *Financial Times* and *People Management* and is the author of two other books, *Mindful Coaching* and *Coaching in Times of Crisis and Transformation*.

D1352281

Liz Hall

# Coach Your Team

**BUSINESS**

PENGUIN BUSINESS

UK | USA | Canada | Ireland | Australia
India | New Zealand | South Africa

Penguin Business is part of the Penguin Random
House group of companies whose addresses can
be found at global.penguinrandomhouse.com.

First published 2019
001

Copyright © Liz Hall, 2019

The moral right of the author has been asserted

Text design by Richard Marston
Set in 11.75/14.75 pt Minion Pro
Typeset by Jouve (UK), Milton Keynes
Printed and bound in Great Britain by
Clays Ltd, Elcograf S.p.A.

A CIP catalogue record for this book is available
from the British Library

ISBN: 978–0–241–39645–2

**Follow us on LinkedIn: linkedin.com/
company/penguinbusiness**

www.greenpenguin.co.uk

I dedicate this book with love and gratitude to my soulmate and husband, Ray. For everything, including your insightful input and support, which helped to keep me sane and to give shape to this book, particularly when I couldn't see the wood for the trees.

To my mindfulness teacher, Thay – your deep wisdom, compassion and ability to bring mindfulness alive will stay with me always.

And to my late daemon dog Ziggy – your loyalty, and your noble sweet gentle energy kept me company for fourteen years, including throughout the writing of this book.

# Contents

List of Figures     ix
List of Tables     x
Introduction     xi

**PART ONE: SETTING OUT**
1 Starting the Journey     3
2 The Research     13
3 Understanding Yourself and Others     30

**PART TWO: MAKING IT HAPPEN**
4 Starting from the Inside Out: Coaching Ourselves     41
5 Coaching One-to-One: Laying the Foundations     44
6 Coaching One-to-One: Building Rapport     57
7 Coaching One-to-One: Facilitating Learning and Results     74
8 Coaching Your Team     102
9 Establishing a Conscious Coaching Culture     135

**PART THREE: TAKING IT FORWARD**
10 Potential Obstacles to Effective Coaching     155
11 Coaching for Stress and Mental Health Problems     159

Afterword: Is the Future Teal?                              166
Acknowledgements                                           169
Appendix 1: Tips for Picking a Coach                       170
Appendix 2: Coaching Programme Planning                    173
Appendix 3: Planning Your Coaching Sessions                176
Endnotes                                                   181
Index                                                      195

# List of Figures

Figure 1: Triangle of Awareness                           9
Figure 2: Listening Levels Bandwidth                      61
Figure 3: The Directive–Non-Directive Spectrum            68

# List of Tables

Table 1: Characteristics of Being and Doing Mind Modes    36
Table 2: Core Conscious Coaching Competencies    55
Table 3: The 'Halos and Horns' Model    96

# Introduction

In 2014, *Harvard Business Review* ran an article on VUCA, the now ubiquitous acronym coined by the US military to describe volatile, uncertain, complex and ambiguous post-Cold War global conditions. The article highlighted how the acronym was fast becoming management shorthand for 'It's crazy out there!' The world was indeed a little crazy then. Around this time, I co-wrote and edited a book about coaching in times of crisis and transformation, prompted in part by the fallout from the 2008 Global Economic Crisis. I remember wondering if the theme would continue to have a shelf life. It would be funny, if it wasn't so serious. The world seems to have become a whole lot crazier.

We're in the midst of a perfect storm of global challenges, including a worldwide crisis in mental well-being. Mental health issues, such as anxiety and depression, are taking an enormous toll on the economy, on individuals and those around them and on people's abilities to contribute meaningfully to the organizations within which they work. In the UK alone, poor mental health is costing employers up to £42 billion a year in lost productivity,[1] absenteeism and 'presenteeism' (where employees feel under pressure to go to work, or work long hours, when they're unwell). In the US, up to $500 billion a year is lost in productivity.[2]

There are many other urgent issues we face in the workplace and society, as leaders/managers and in our organizations. The list is vast. Climate change and related issues – such as increasing numbers of refugees, food insecurity, and the threat of the Sixth Mass Extinction. Growing wealth disparity and the erosion of the middle class. Rising nationalism. Declining trust in institutions and leaders – attendees at the World Economic Forum (WEF) in Davos in January 2019 underlined a widespread lack of faith (including in government). Bombardment with data, manipulation via social media platforms and a rise in human disconnection as technology becomes a common substitute for direct contact. Ethical concerns, disruption of business models, and an urgent need for reskilling coupled with widespread redundancy, as new technologies including Artificial Intelligence become widely adopted in the Fourth Industrial Revolution. And unless managed wisely, the significant transformations in global labour markets will increase already widening skills gaps, inequality and polarization, the WEF has warned.[3]

Individually and collectively, faced with all these challenges, we need to wake up.[4] We need new types of conversations. We need new collective narratives and practices – about how we show up with one another, how we work together, how we lead, follow and manage others, about what it means to be human in these times.

Leaders and managers have a pivotal role to play in seeing off the old practices which no longer work for us, creating and putting in place alternatives that are more readily fit for purpose. We must create new processes that align around meaning, purpose and values and which draw on and foster courage, creativity, community, compassion and cooperation. Ones that honour the authenticity and diversity that movements such as #MeToo and #BlackLivesMatter have brought to our attention.

Many of us – in our roles as leaders, managers and coaches, in our organizations and our lives in general – are seeking change. We're searching for alternative ways of doing things and of being. Because, on some level, we know things can't carry on as they are. It's just not sustainable. The huge growth globally in coaching and the adoption of mindfulness in all sorts of areas – including the workplace, education, and even politics – are, in part, a response to the challenges we face.

It was a recognition that I couldn't continue as I was that led me to mindfulness, years before I'd started working as a coach. It was a time when I was extremely stressed and worn down, a single mother, working very hard as a journalist – ironically writing lots about well-being at work. (An irony not lost on me at the time, although I don't recall having the energy or desire to laugh at my situation!) I had a very young baby (now all grown up) who I was reluctantly taking to childcare, and I felt very torn. I never seemed to have enough time, energy or patience.

One day, driving home from the childminder, my daughter screaming, I snapped. I pulled over and I screamed too.

A woman tapped on the car window. 'Are you okay? Would you like to come in for a cup of tea?'

Gulping back tears, and feeling ashamed, I nodded.

What a lovely woman! I've often remembered her with deep gratitude. She reassured me – she was a working mother of four – that she'd had her struggles too, on many an occasion.

After tea, biscuits and the love of a stranger, I drove home. And in floods of tears, I talked to a friend, who happened to be a nurse involved in counselling in general practice. She told me about an approach that was helping her. Although I didn't know it then, it was mindfulness. Not necessarily easy, but so simple. Using that approach, I began to get a glimpse of calmness every now and then, a sense of spaciousness on the odd occasion, a snatch of what it feels like to be in the present, rather than panicking about future deadlines, delivering on projects, how on earth I was going to get everything done, what an awful mother I was. I remember looking at a picture book with my daughter and noticing that, wow, I was actually *with* her. How amazing was that!

Mindfulness and coaching and the many beautiful and meaningful encounters I've had as a result are helping me to wake up, to live and work more consciously, with more purpose. We *need* to wake up and, in many quarters, we *are* waking up.

We are seeing more organizations become purpose-led and driven by conscious leaders as well as in response to shifts in demands, desires, needs and expectations from employees. Increasingly, in addition to the desire and need for support around well-being and mental health, people want work to be about more than just receiving a pay cheque. They want more empowering and facilitative workplace cultures, leadership and management styles. They want meaning and purpose, and development opportunities. Millennials examine organizational values and development opportunities before they choose an employer[5] and particularly want professional development support in the form of coaching and mentoring.[6]

Executive coaching has become a worldwide phenomenon, used to:

- increase resilience and the ability to manage stress
- develop higher emotional intelligence
- increase flexibility and openness
- shift culture, and
- create new narratives.

Increasing numbers of organizations now offer coaching internally, and growing numbers are developing a coaching culture, training up their own internal coaches, and weaving coaching into leadership development. Coaching is considered a key leadership responsibility[7] and a core leadership competency, distinguishing outstanding leaders from those with average abilities in their field.

Mindfulness too is everywhere. Google, EY, the armed forces and many other employers have rolled out mindfulness programmes. It's being introduced in schools all over the world. In the healthcare arena, it's become one of the go-to therapies for recurrent depression and a host of other mental and physical conditions.

Mindfulness is helping those I work with in my coaching practice be more resilient, better able to work with complexity and ambiguity. They are more creative, emotionally intelligent, and have more mental clarity, resulting in vastly enhanced relationships with themselves and others. Ultimately, mindfulness helps those I work with to be much happier, which arguably is the most important benefit of all.

Mindfulness is perfect for these challenging times. A recent study of leaders who had trained in mindfulness found that they were more resilient, more collaborative and better able to lead in complex conditions.[8] It also recognized that the benefits enjoyed by mindful leaders and managers had rippled out through the rest of the organization.

Many organizations are recognizing the benefits of mindful coaching and adopting the practice within their structures and processes. Whilst mindfulness and coaching are separate interventions, they can be combined or offered alongside one another in various ways to great effect, especially if supported by initiatives to build compassion. It's what I call Conscious Coaching.

The Conscious Coaching approach draws on years of my own and others' research, and a wealth of experiences and learning from working with coaching clients, teaching mindfulness and compassion, and editing the magazine *Coaching at Work*. It combines both ancient disciplines, such as mindfulness, and new fields, such as neuroscience, as we increasingly have access to an ever-growing collection of tried-and-tested, evidence-based and cutting-edge discoveries, practices and techniques. In this book I will introduce and explain some of these for you to build into your own organization.

First, *Coach Your Team* examines the *why* of mindful coaching by examining the research, which highlights the many benefits of the practice. Second, the *what* – what do we mean by a leader, manager or organization adopting Conscious Coaching? Finally, the *how*, providing practical guidance on how to put Conscious Coaching in place for you and others in your team.

Of course, whilst there's an order to the book, you're free to dip in and out as best serves you on your own journey. The content is presented to enable you to easily do so. My intention as your guide in this book is to sow some positive seeds to support awakening, growth, more conscious working, and the fostering of workplaces in which all can flourish.

It's down to you which seeds you decide to water!

I bow to you.

Liz Hall

# PART ONE

Setting Out

# 1  Starting the Journey

Increasingly, we're seeing the term 'conscious' used in relation to leadership, coaching, companies, capitalism, to pretty much everything these days. The concept of waking up, becoming aware, and realizing we need to change our ways of thinking and being is very much part of the zeitgeist. Building greater awareness, and thus increased choice, followed by informed change, is fundamental to the Conscious Coaching approach.

As mindfulness and compassion become more mainstream and their benefits better understood, we're seeing a rise in the numbers of coaches, leaders and managers adopting a coaching style which draws on these approaches. Conscious Coaching explicitly embraces both. But, what do we mean by coaching in general, mindfulness, compassion and Conscious Coaching?

## What is coaching?

> 'Coaching is partnering with clients in a thought-provoking and creative process that inspires them to maximize their personal and professional potential.'
> – International Coach Federation[1]

In the workplace, coaching is about enabling employees to take self-responsibility. It's about empowering them to find their own solutions and make their own decisions, and assumes that they are capable of this. Thus, I define coaching as:

A co-created process to help people tap into their own wisdom so they can learn, grow and fulfil their potential.

Coaching can be delivered one-to-one, in groups and in teams. We can also coach ourselves. Team and group coaching are no longer the new kids on the block. Companies such as PwC have been delivering team coaching for many years, others have taken longer to catch up, but they're catching up fast. A 2016 report found that over the following three years, 76 per cent of organizations were planning to increase team coaching and 47 per cent of organizations were considering introducing group coaching.[2]

However, many confuse team coaching with other team activities such as action learning sets, facilitation, team building, process consulting, or team away-days. It's important to understand the difference.

- **Team coaching** is a collective intervention for groups of people who work together in a team, using core coaching skills and paying attention to group dynamics.
- **Group coaching** is individual coaching in a group setting.

Coaching can take place informally, such as a 'corridor coaching'-style brief conversation between a manager and a direct report, or it can be more formal. The essential skills – such as active listening and asking, not telling – are the same.

## How is coaching different from other interventions?

### Coaching versus therapy or counselling

Coaching in general is often informed by therapeutic approaches including Cognitive Behavioural Therapy, Solution Focused Therapy and Transactional Analysis. However, coaching differs from therapy and counselling as we assume those being coached are well enough to solve their own problems, albeit with coaching support at first. This doesn't necessarily rule out working with people who are struggling with their mental health, feeling overwhelmed or anxious, for example.

### Coaching versus mentoring

Coaching and mentoring are sometimes confused as there is a crossover in the skills used by the coach and the mentor (such as active listening). However, with mentoring, we assume the mentor has valuable expertise and experience to share. In coaching, we assume the other person knows what's best for them.

### Coaching versus training

With training, as with mentoring, we assume there's knowledge to impart, and the trainer 'owns' the process and drives the curriculum. In coaching, the person being coached 'owns' the process.

## What is Conscious Coaching?

Conscious Coaching is built on the core concepts and competencies underpinning professional coaching, which we will look at later on, combined with the philosophies and practices of mindfulness and compassion. We can define it thus:

> Conscious Coaching is a process combining core coaching skills and techniques with the fields of mindfulness and compassion to help people tap into their own wisdom so they can learn, grow and fulfil their potential.

But what do we mean by mindfulness and compassion, and where do these come from?

## A very short history of mindfulness

Mindfulness is an ancient technique that has stood the test of time. Its roots are in Buddhist teachings from the historical Buddha (the term means 'awakened one') who lived more than 2,500 years ago in the region now known as Nepal.

There is a history of contemplation in all the major religions. However, relatively new is the spread of mindfulness into a wide range of secular contexts.

Jon Kabat-Zinn is one of the leading figures in spreading mindfulness beyond the spiritual setting. In 1979, in the basement of the University of Massachusetts Medical Center in the US, he began offering the first eight-week Mindfulness-Based Stress Reduction programme, drawing on yoga, t'ai chi and Zen Buddhism. This programme has gone on to inspire variations and adaptations across the globe, including in education, the workplace and psychotherapy. In the United Kingdom, for example, advisory public body the National Institute for Health and Clinical Excellence (NICE) has recommended

Mindfulness-Based Cognitive Therapy for recurrent depression since 2004. Given its role in healthcare, mindfulness has been subjected to many studies, and as such is now considered to have a respected stamp of approval.

Kabat-Zinn defines mindfulness as:

The intention to pay attention in a particular way: on purpose, in the present moment, and non-judgmentally.[3]

The UK's Mental Health Foundation[4] acknowledges the body component of mindfulness in its definition: 'Mindfulness is an integrative, mind-body based approach that helps people change the way they think and feel about their experiences.'

UK policy institute the Mindfulness Initiative highlights that it's 'an inherent human capacity akin to language acquisition; a capacity that enables people to focus on what they experience in the moment, inside themselves as well as in their environment, with an attitude of openness, curiosity and care.'[5]

Other attitudes associated with mindfulness include non-judgement and acceptance.

Ellen Langer, a prolific researcher on mindfulness, defines mindfulness as a 'flexible state of mind in which we are actively engaged in the present, noticing new things and sensitive to context'.[6]

Practising formal meditation is just one of many ways to get into a 'mindful state'. Other ways include going for a 'mindful walk' or engaging in team activities specifically designed to promote mindful traits such as flexibility and openness.

Mindfulness is best experienced to fully understand it.

## Try this: Getting mindful

Sitting[7] for the next five minutes or so somewhere you won't be disturbed, getting comfortable, loosening your shoulders, resting your hands in your lap. Sitting upright in a 'dignified', erect posture. Closing your eyes or gazing downwards. Noticing where your body makes contact with the seat, your feet with the ground. Taking three deep breaths, then breathing normally.

Noticing the sounds around you. Just listening, not feeling like you have to do anything about them, not even labelling them. Noticing sounds coming and going. Then 'coming back' into the room and opening your eyes.

We will come back to this practice at the beginning of many of the exercises that follow throughout the book, so make sure you're comfortable doing it.

### The Triangle of Awareness

Another way of getting mindful is to work with the Triangle of Awareness[8] (Figure 1), a map of territory we explore in mindfulness. It involves us engaging in the moment *in here* with what's *in here* and *out there*. It invites us to shine the spotlight of awareness on to whatever we notice in our field of awareness – maybe the sunlight streaming through the window, the pouring rain, some beautiful flowers, someone's smile or grimace. We become aware of our thoughts, emotions and bodily sensations – which are connected.

**Figure 1: Triangle of Awareness (thoughts / emotions / bodily sensations)**

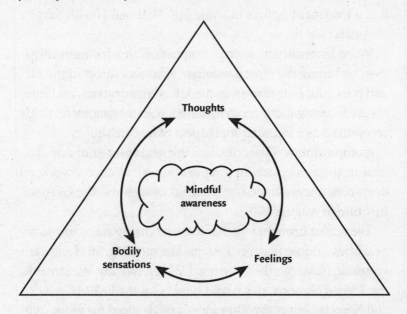

## A very short history of compassion

Like mindfulness, compassion has long been associated with spirituality. It's deemed a core virtue in all the world's major religions. However, again like mindfulness, more recently it's been rippling beyond the spiritual context into fields such as healthcare, education and the workplace, including in coaching. As with mindfulness, the adoption of compassion within the healthcare arena and the increasing number of studies on its impact have done much to 'legitimize' the practice within a secular context. Clinical psychologist Paul Gilbert is one of the pioneers in bringing this about. He developed Compassion Focused Therapy (CFT) to treat clients with severe mental health problems. The scope of application of CFT has been widened to treat other conditions including chronic pain, and it is a treatment option in some UK National Health Service hospitals.

We're increasingly seeing compassion in education initiatives including the Compassionate Schools Project in the US, and the CoEd Foundation in the UK. Organizations and leaders are focusing more on compassion, with it being increasingly recognized as a foundational aspect of leadership.

Compassion was described as 'the next frontier of mindfulness in the workplace' in a report published after a weekend deep-dive retreat hosted by Mindful Leader and the Garrison Institute in August 2018.

The retreat brought together internal champions of mindfulness from Google, BuzzFeed, Aetna, Harvard Pilgrim Healthcare, Humana, Novo Nordisk, Boeing, LVMH, Fidelity Investments, the United Nations, the World Bank, Goodwill, YMCA USA and Naropa University. They identified the need for more compassionate conversations about difficult topics at work, and that compassion can help with the stress and difficulties of change management. From the retreat emerged a call for compassion and empathy to be built into leadership development, laying the foundations with mindfulness.

One way to define compassion is 'empathy with action'. Certainly the action part is key.

Paul Gilbert defines it as:

The sensitivity to suffering in ourselves and others, combined with the sincere wish to relieve it.[9]

Physician and founder of the Academy of Health Coaching Tim Anstiss points out that it's not one thing: it's 'a complex, innate, motivational, interpersonal and behavioural system . . . it depends on and is enabled by a range of skills and competencies, abilities and strengths including empathy; sympathy; generosity; openness; distress tolerance; commitment and courage.'[10]

International leadership institute Roffey Park has carried out extensive research into compassion at work, developing a Compassion at Work Index which helps individuals assess their level of compassion at work. It defines five attributes in relation to compassion.

- Being empathetic
- Being 'alive to the suffering of others'
- Being non-judgemental
- Tolerating personal distress
- Taking appropriate action[11]

We often think of compassion in terms of us extending it to others but it's also about giving it to ourselves (self-compassion) and receiving compassion.

## The conscious leader or manager-as-coach

So having explored what we mean by coaching, mindfulness and compassion, let's now look at what a leader or manager who draws on the Conscious Coaching approach would look like.

### Qualities, attributes and aspirations
- Is resilient, adaptable and flexible
- Is self-aware and emotionally intelligent
- Is empathetic and compassionate

- Aspires to be non-judgemental
- Is humble
- Is curious and open
- Is creative and open to experimentation
- Has access to metacognition (being aware of being aware)
- Can sit with ambiguity or 'not-knowing'

## Behaviours

- Has trained in and regularly practises developing mindfulness and compassion
- Has an understanding of coaching skills for themselves and others
- Embodies compassion by taking action to alleviate others' suffering and encouraging others to do likewise
- Encourages others to be curious, creative and open to experimentation
- Contributes to developing teams and organizational culture rooted in coaching, mindfulness and compassion

# 2  The Research

> 'Companies that don't harness coaching are not only missing out on a powerful tool for organizational change and employee engagement, but also one that boosts productivity.'
> – Nick Cutland, director of quality at City & Guilds and ILM[1]

A review of studies investigating separately the potential benefits of introducing coaching, mindfulness and compassion reveals plenty of common ground between the three. The research points to a number of key benefits arising from engaging in any of these practices (and one might assume that engaging in all three would increase the impact).

- **Resilience** and well-being
- **Emotional intelligence:** greater self-awareness and awareness of others, improving relationships, fostering collaboration and resolving conflict
- **Productivity:** improving individual and collective performance through increased trust, greater employee engagement, greater creativity and big-picture thinking
- **Agile leadership:** cultivating a more adaptive, agile and collaborative leadership or management style

- **Implementing change:** bringing about systemic change and implementing a coaching culture

Let's explore these in turn.

## Resilience

Many studies point to coaching's potential for building resilience, improving mental and physical health and well-being by helping people manage stress better, amongst other benefits.[2,3]

One study, by Anthony Grant and Sean O'Connor,[4] highlights how coaching helps people be more resilient, and more 'change ready'– more agile, more confident in dealing with change and turbulence, and more oriented towards learning.

Coaching can be a 'just-in-time' intervention, helping employees avoid becoming depressed and taking time off from work.

In the current climate in which many fear they'll lose their jobs, people feel immense pressure to be seen to be performing well. However, over-working doesn't increase productivity, and much research proves the opposite. Presenteeism has been associated with a greater loss in productivity than absenteeism.[5] Studies reveal a tipping point when it comes to how much overtime we can 'get away with'. If we work more than 55 hours a week, our risk of stroke is 33 per cent higher than for those working 35–40 hours a week.[6]

During coaching sessions, we can challenge unhelpful assumptions that many employees are beholden to, which threaten their productivity but also their well-being and perhaps even their lives. Assumptions including: 'I'm a much better person if I keep busy all the time', 'I must do everything perfectly' and 'I must be seen to be working extremely hard otherwise people will think I'm worthless.'

Coaching can support employees already experiencing poor mental health, which is more common than we might think. Behind closed doors, many of my clients and those of other coaches I talk to share how they're struggling more and more. One client, Joseph, is very typical: 'I feel like I'm hanging on by a thread. The demands feel relentless.'

Coaching can support people to develop personalized strategies to overcome their problems whilst 'normalizing' their experiences so they don't feel alone. It offers a safe confidential space in which employees can explore difficult feelings, thoughts and symptoms, particularly if they are resistant to having therapy or to using an Employee Assistance Programme (EAP). In one study, although 23 per cent of employees said they had access to an EAP, just 2 per cent had used it during their most recent instances of mental ill health.[7]

Mindfulness has been shown to improve all sorts of mental and physical health conditions, including anxiety and insomnia, type 2 diabetes, cardiovascular disease, asthma and chronic pain.[8]

Combining coaching with mindfulness training can be very effective. One study[9] found that mindfulness training (MT) combined with coaching helps clients attain their health-related goals, particularly if they receive MT first. Some 45 participants were randomly assigned to three health programmes: MT followed by cognitive-behavioural solution-focused (CB-SF) coaching; CB-SF coaching followed by MT; and health education seminars. Those who had received MT before coaching reported significant decreases in anxiety and stress. The study underlined the effectiveness of the facilitative style on which coaching is built, finding that greater behaviour change was achieved through facilitation and support than by education and persuasion.

Research suggests that actively developing compassion also boosts health and well-being, reducing depression and anxiety[10] and improving ability to cope with adversity.[11] It helps to increase happiness and optimism[12] and improves levels of positive emotions such as gratitude.[13] And it can increase staff retention, as Appletree's story shows.

## CASE STUDY

### Appletree Answers

John Ratliff started telephone answering service Appletree Answers in 1995 from a two-bedroom apartment in Delaware in the US. By 2012, when he sold the company to a strategic buyer, he'd grown the company organically and through a series of acquisitions to a 650-strong workforce, with 24 US locations. Compassion has played a part in the business's success.

While still President and CEO, he and his team introduced a compassion-based initiative called Dream On in a bid to strengthen employee engagement and build a meaningful company culture. The scheme, inspired by the Make a Wish Foundation approach, allowed employees to regularly express compassion to each other by helping them make a lifetime dream a reality. One asked for a birthday party in a circus for his daughter, another for her husband who was undergoing chemotherapy to watch his favourite team's match in the stadium.[14]

In a video on the scheme,[15] John says, 'You go back in the history of your company and you look for moments that were game-changing or pivotal. It's one of those moments we can look at and say, wow, our company changed that day, forever.'

In the same video, employees share how touched they were by their experiences and how they felt much more loyal to the company as a result. Within six months of introducing Dream On, staff turnover dropped from 97 per cent to 33 per cent – pretty extraordinary, as call centres have extremely low retention rates.

John has gone on to co-found align5, a company which serves growth company entrepreneurs, where he leads strategic initiatives, and coaches.

Compassion is now part of Appletree Answers' language. For example, its promotion material states that its 'call handling experts combine a compassionate interaction with best-in-class technology'. Coaching plays a part too – call centre employees receive frequent feedback from dedicated managers and coaching in accuracy, professionalism, grammar and tone.

Dream On is a legacy John remains proud of, and align5 offers support to companies that wish to implement the initiative. In the video, John says, 'It's changed me fundamentally, to be that in touch with what our people have to go through sometimes . . . this concept of Dream On, and where companies get involved in bettering the lives of their employees, if that could be my legacy, then my career would have been a success.'

---

## Emotional intelligence

Emotional intelligence (EQ) is an important skill in workplace performance[16] both individually, predicting individuals' leadership behaviours,[17] and on a group level, with higher leader EQ levels associated with higher levels of group effectiveness.[18,19] No wonder that boosting EQ in and of itself is a widely held objective in coaching, particularly in leadership and management coaching.

Research suggests that coaching boosts EQ and improves relationships, although it needs time to embed. One study by Anthony Grant[20] compared outcomes from two programmes: one with 23 participants going through a 13-week coaching skills training course comprising weekly workshops (lasting two and a half hours) and action learning; the other with 20 participants completing a two-day Manager-as-Coach training programme, with a three-week action learning break between days one and two. Participation in the longer course delivered increases in both goal-focused coaching skills and emotional intelligence, whereas the two-day block intensive training was associated with increased goal-focused coaching skills, but not emotional intelligence.

Improving relationships helps to reduce workplace conflict[21] which can have substantial negative effects for individuals and organizations.[22] Widespread stress, organizational restructuring (and the accompanying uncertainty and threat to status and security) and changes to modern working practices (with more remote working and working on-the-go increasing the amount of online communication), all contribute to creating conflict. We all know how easy it is to get things wrong in emails, for example. High levels of relationship conflict can lower morale and productivity, and increase staff turnover, all of which impact organizational profitability.

Mindfulness is highly effective at boosting EQ. At least 45 workplace mindfulness research studies have linked mindfulness to improved relationships at work, supporting collaboration and improving employees' resilience in the face of challenges. Mindfulness delivers improvements in all four pillars of EQ – self-awareness, self-management, social awareness and relationship management – leading to reductions in workplace conflict.[23,24]

Studies in the US found that after mindfulness training, there were improvements in emotional intelligence metrics, which included decision-making skills. They also included resistance to bias, including racial bias and age-related stereotyping. One study on the judiciary found that a brief mindfulness intervention reduced reliance on assumptions based on gender or race in assessments about reoffending, as well as increasing focus, attention and reflection during decision-making processes.[25]

Employees of leaders who practise mindfulness are more likely to show concern towards co-workers and express opinions honestly, according to one study.[26]

Developing compassion improves relationships – increasing collaboration,[27] trust and connections with others at work,[28] increasing relationship satisfaction,[29,30] promoting healing and building the quality of relationships, and strengthening shared values of interconnectedness in organizations.[31]

## Productivity

Coaching is widely seen as integral to productivity and performance. According to a 2018 survey by the Institute of Leadership & Management,[32] boosting confidence, performance and productivity were the most important positive changes witnessed by those receiving coaching – not just for themselves but for their team and organization. Some 58 per cent of respondents reported higher confidence after coaching, and 42 per cent saw an improvement in performance in colleagues who had been coached. This in turn meant an upturn in performance of the entire team. A huge majority of respondents said that coaching would have helped them during periods of struggle when managing an individual (84 per cent) and with a particular project (88 per cent).

Sustained team coaching can deliver sustainable and lasting improvements to team performance, more so than team bonding and team building exercises, according to research.[33,34]

## CASE STUDY

### Legal & General

Embedding coaching into British multinational financial services firm Legal & General's talent development programme improved retention, employee engagement and performance. Evaluation found that customer satisfaction had risen by 15 per cent, staff satisfaction by 20 per cent. In addition, 80 per cent of call quality scores improved month on month over a 12-month period, and there were improvements in individual performance measures in months when managers were delivering monthly coaching sessions.[35]

The programme focuses on developing a coaching culture and is oversubscribed. Managers at all levels are involved as mentors, coaches and project buddies, either delivering part of the programme or encouraging team members to sign up.

Staff promotion has increased and the programme is contributing to a significant shift in the learning and development culture. Since 2014, more than 80 per cent of graduates have progressed in their careers, with more than 50 per cent being promoted into a team manager role.[36]

Increased productivity was one of the commonly cited outcomes from coaching, along with improved communication skills and increased self-esteem/self-confidence, according to another study from the ICF.[37]

Mindfulness also improves productivity. Employees of leaders who practise mindfulness feel less exhausted, and have better work–life balance and job performance ratings.[38] Mindfulness boosts productivity by enabling greater cognitive flexibility,[39] faster, more rational decisions and strategic thinking,[40] and promoting creativity and insight in problem solving.[41] Employers rolling out mindfulness to boost creativity and innovation include Apple, Google, McKinsey, Proctor & Gamble, General Mills and Target. Developing compassion increases creativity too.[42]

One way coaching boosts team and organizational performance is by increasing employee engagement. Employees are more likely to be engaged if they are led by compassionate leaders[43] while developing a compassionate culture increases employees' commitment to the organization and decreases their likelihood of leaving.[44,45]

CASE STUDY

## Boots Contract Manufacturing

Growing leaders as development coaches helped global contract manufacturing business Boots Contract Manufacturing (BCM) retain 92 per cent of its talent, enhancing their roles and saving an estimated £88,000 in recruitment costs.

BCM engaged leaders in workshops on self-awareness, energizing strengths and empowering talent, and creating a bespoke development plan. Janine Goodwin, then senior learning and development manager at BCM, said of the first workshop, 'The focus was to get leaders to recognize the traditional authoritarian culture that existed in some areas, and understand and embrace the opportunities that a more coaching style of leadership could bring in developing talent.'

Leaders reported feeling empowered, confident in coaching, demonstrating more coaching skills, such as listening more and asking more questions. BCM now develops through a coaching leadership style, which 'starts from understanding what employees care about and what energises them'.[46]

## Agile leadership

Coaching is often introduced to help leaders and managers shift their style from command-and-control to collaborative and facilitative. Coaching helps leaders become 'transformational leaders' who build a shared purpose with employees, including by inspiring and innovating,[47,48] and whose approach includes promoting self-development in all and engaging others in a cooperative and affiliative manner.[49]

As leadership coaches and consultants Erik de Haan and Anthony Kasozi have written,[50] coaching helps leaders and managers become more self-aware so they can:

- understand their vulnerabilities
- balance their strengths and weaknesses
- become more compassionate
- truly focus on the team, and
- become more resilient.

It offers leaders and managers a reflective space where they can explore their role and the ever-shifting challenges in the wider field, as Simon Cavicchia and Maria Gilbert have noted.[51]

Mindfulness boosts leaders' ability to lead in complex and challenging times. One way it does this is by boosting self-awareness and thus the ability to challenge personal assumptions and to access multiple perspectives, helping teams avoid 'groupthink' (where teams come up with unchallenged and poor-quality group-wide thinking and decision making). It also increases ethical and sustainable decision making and behaviour[52,53] and helps people to become more in touch with their true values.[54]

Research by Ashridge[55] found 'mindful leaders' were better able to collaborate and lead in complex conditions, becoming more willing to stay put in the face of difficulty, and more likely to proactively promote emergent, bottom-up decisions. Key was the development of three meta-capacities:

- metacognition (being aware of being aware)
- allowing (letting whatever *is* the case *be* the case, meeting our experiences with a spirit of openness and kindness to ourselves and others), and
- curiosity.

Developing these enabled greater focus, emotional regulation, perspective taking, empathy and adaptability, helping the leaders create more space for more adaptive responses.

Iñigo Castillo fits the category of conscious leader-as-coach perfectly, although he'd beg to differ as he's already embodying a core mindfulness attitude of humility! His story shows that, even if you're a lone voice, if you're leading the show, you can have a dramatic impact. I'm reminded of the words of Taoist philosopher Lao Tzu (born 601 BC): 'A leader is best when people barely know she or he exists. When the work is done, her or his aim fulfilled, people will say, "We did it ourselves."'

CASE STUDY

## Iñigo Castillo's story

Iñigo Castillo, CEO of Renolit Chile, credits his mindfulness practice, training as a coach and participative leadership approach with helping to turn Renolit Hispania around while CEO from March 2005 to December 2016. Renolit is an international manufacturer of high-quality plastic films and derived products.

'The profit and loss accounts show that introducing mindfulness generates good results. I'm sure if I hadn't drawn on mindfulness, the business wouldn't have been able to get over the great crisis it had. Mindfulness helped the firm greatly, in this case having a CEO who could lead and direct crisis change,' he told me.[56]

Iñigo first started meditating and coaching in 2012 and he's experienced many personal benefits. They have helped him work on his ego, and therefore promote creativity and innovation. 'When you realize that your ego is your mind, and that to get to know it you need mindfulness, and your attitude and behaviour at work begin to take your ego into account, you start to open up more completely to other people, and [it becomes easier] to innovate. You ask other people constant questions. Why don't we do this? What would happen if?'

He believes coaching and leadership go hand in hand. 'Everyone can generate their own best ideas. I used to try to solve everything, I'd ask but wouldn't let people answer! Now I let them think. It's fantastic, much better for motivation, people feel more important, you lead the search but everyone comes up with their own ideas. The leader-coach style is definitely beneficial for the business.'

Although Iñigo has found both mindfulness and coaching beneficial, he's discovered not everyone is open to them. He offered coaching to thirty middle managers but only a handful took it up. 'Resistance was perhaps through ignorance or fear. Maybe it just wasn't the right moment.' After all, before 2012, he hadn't understood mindfulness himself, and he too would have been sceptical, he admits.

Iñigo carved out a different way of leading, with a leader-as-coach style. Every January he would hold open, facilitative business-wide meetings reviewing the previous year and looking at next steps. One year, he brought in psychologists to offer mini-workshops on happiness and optimism.

'I think some people thought I was mad! Because of my style, I'm seen as an *avis raris* [strange bird]. I've discovered that when you generate this kind of personal transformation through mindfulness, for example, you're seen differently.'

However, 'Even though there was low commitment to some of the initiatives I introduced, I think the sum of them was significant to bring about cultural change. In comparison with 2006, by 2016 we had more flexible working practices, better team working, less conflict between leaders and bosses, and better communication. And I think this was achieved because of the example set by leadership which was a much more innovative modern leadership, paying more attention to people.

'In business, the final results are measurable economically and it's clear coaching and mindfulness deliver results and I am happy about where we got to.'

## Matthew Runeckles' story

Matthew Runeckles, deputy head of investment bank operations and technology in Société Générale's Global Solution Centre, has also drawn on mindfulness and coaching, helping him land a desired role and to create a strong trust-based team.

In just three and a half years, Matthew Runeckles went from being in charge of around 100 people to overseeing around 4,600 and taking on additional responsibilities.

He attributes his success in his role (as well as getting it in the first place) to coaching and mindfulness. They have helped him create a strong team around him in which trust, vulnerability and accountability are the currencies.

Matthew was first assigned a coach, Ram Ramanathan from leadership development firm Coacharaya, when promoted from head of a function to senior management, increasing the number of people reporting to him from around 170 to around 330.

The coaching supported Matthew in developing and adopting a personal-coaching style of leadership, exploring values, beliefs, attitudes and behaviours. 'Behind that exploration was the concept that to be a good leader, you have to be passionate and motivated to be able to drag people along with you.

'Through the coaching, I moved more towards getting my employees to give their own solutions.'

Matthew explored where he wanted to be in two decades' time in terms of different areas of his life – health, wealth, learning, relationships, spirituality and so on. Ram encouraged him to meditate and visualize what it would be like if the dream came true. Then, in September 2018, the CEO left and was replaced by the deputy. Ram encouraged him to visualize getting the role he wanted. 'Ram had a strong belief that it would work as he's done it with thousands of people.' Matthew was successful in landing the role.

In addition, mindfulness has 'helped me be more present and more able to focus on what I'm doing at any given time. It helps you be more engaged when you listen. You have the right body language, demonstrating that you're listening without judging. It's about being curious. I wouldn't say I'm perfect at it but it helps me understand [others'] perspectives and therefore make better decisions.'

Convinced of the many benefits, including for well-being, he employed a mindfulness coach to train his management team in basic mindfulness skills too. He's meditated with his team and tried coaching exercises at a half-day event gathering those in his immediate senior management team, direct reports and the HR manager.

Benefits for the team have included creating more trust, which helps the team be more successful.

'To build a strong team environment, you need to create trust, which is created by people feeling safe, and safety is created by people feeling vulnerable with each other.'

---

## Implementing change

Organizational change, brought about by restructures, mergers, office moves or changes in leadership, is part of the experience of belonging to a large, modern organization.

Since 2000, the rate and unpredictability of change has escalated[57] significantly, bringing yet greater demands on managers and leaders as well as others. Coaching can be immensely helpful in handling the turbulence that these changes bring.

The ICF has found that coaching is *the* most helpful activity in achieving the goals of change management initiatives,[58] according to a 2018 survey of HR practitioners and leaders. Another 2018 study[59] highlighted the positive contribution of coaching during organizational change. The Institute of Leadership & Management surveyed more than 1,000 UK professionals working in healthcare, finance or retail. The majority (76 per cent) believe coaching is helpful during such times, and that coaching can support teams when adopting new technology and different ways of working (79 per cent).

According to the ICF/HCI report, coaching is 'a powerful tool to support individuals, teams and organizations to explore resistance, enhance communication and promote resilience in the face of change'.[60] It found that companies with strong coaching cultures were more likely to be successful at large-scale strategic change and other outcomes associated with being a high-performing organization.

Coaching can reduce or remove fear, increasing openness to change. As the Institute of Leadership & Management's report says, 'Coaching is the most nuanced of L&D interventions and as such can help members of the workforce to understand that change can be good and can help shift their mindset from a negative one to a positive one. It can remove the fear factor from change and help individuals transition mentally and practically.'[61]

Research by Anthony Grant and Sean O'Connor[62] highlights how coaching helps to boost solution-focused thinking, a key skill in times of organizational turbulence and change.

**CASE STUDY**

## News UK

News UK, formerly News International, was rocked by a telephone hacking and police bribery scandal in 2011. In response, it set in motion a raft of initiatives to heal and transform its culture, rebuilding confidence and boosting engagement, including an internal coaching initiative.

One of the internal coaches, Jon Moorhead, said in 2014, 'What happened here was absolutely devastating and there are still a lot of scars . . . Coaching is part of the resurrection of the company.'[63]

As well as playing a part in healing, internal coaching aimed to equip employees to adapt to the ever-changing media landscape.

In 2016, James Hutton, then head of talent and development at News UK, shared how coaching was helping to retain talent in the wake of the scandal, and that the coaching culture was growing, with coaching increasingly being used with teams.

# 3  Understanding Yourself and Others

Psychological awareness is key to excellent coaching. Deepening our understanding of how our brains, bodies and emotions work empowers us to coach ourselves and others with empathy, finding positive strategies and behaviours to move forward. So much of what we do at work is defined by our relationships, so being tuned in to how others may be feeling is a vital element of being a leader or manager-as-coach.

Below is a curation of some of the up-to-date thinking that has informed coaching, mindfulness and compassion practice. Being aware of these concepts will give you an informed grounding in the foundation of Conscious Coaching practice.

## The gift of neuroplasticity

> 'We are what we repeatedly do. Excellence, then, is not an act, but a habit.'
> – Aristotle[1]

One of the greatest discoveries from neuroscience is that of our brain's plasticity, even once we hit adulthood. When we repeatedly engage in new behaviours or thinking patterns, we create new or strengthen existing neural pathways.[2] Conscious Coaching puts this capacity to excellent use.

A 2013 study using brain-imaging technology indicated that different coaching styles activate different brain networks and regions.[3] Coaching people around their dreams and visions, as we do in Conscious Coaching – rather than for compliance – is more likely to activate neural mechanisms, the study found. This encouraged the individual to be motivated, willing to tackle difficulties, and open to new ideas and big-picture thinking.

The practice of mindfulness, which is core to Conscious Coaching, also positively impacts our brains by increasing activity in brain regions associated with learning and memory processes, emotion regulation, self-referential processing and perspective taking.[4]

Mindfulness[5] and coaching[6] both boost activity of the prefrontal cortex (PFC), helping to keep it 'online'. The PFC is the seat of our executive functioning; involved in planning, organizing, regulating attention, decision making, getting motivated, how we express our personality and moderating social behaviour.

## How our body, mind and emotions are connected

There's an unhelpful tendency, particularly in the workplace, to prioritize what goes on in our heads and neglect our bodies and emotions, whether that's slouching over our keyboards all day, eating at our desks, or bottling up difficult emotions and allowing stress to build up – or all of the above.

In reality, our minds, bodies and emotions can't be separated and are continuously exchanging information. Recent research shows that in addition to our skull-based brain, we have a smaller brain-like structure in our gut and another in our heart.[7,8] By tuning more into our bodies, which we do in Conscious Coaching, we access wisdom that can serve us and those we coach by precluding mental health problems, building valid relationships and improving workplace dynamics within your organization.

The body offers a powerful crucible for change if we know how to work with it. As Mark Williams and Danny Penman point out in their excellent book, *Mindfulness: a practical guide to finding peace in a frantic world*, 'research shows us that our whole outlook on life can be shifted by tiny changes in the body. Something as subtle as frowning, smiling or altering posture can have a dramatic impact on mood and the type of thoughts flickering across the mind.'[9]

## Try this: Mini body scan[10]

### 10 Minutes

- **Step 1**
  Setting a 10-minute timer, use the practice outlined on page 8, 'Getting mindful', to get into an intentioned mindset for the exercise.
- **Step 2**
  Slowly 'scanning' your body from your toes to the top of your head for any particularly noticeable sensations. Using your total focus and shifting your internal spotlight on each of your body parts, moving upwards through the body. Alternating zooming in to take in

granular detail – for example, what is going on in your left big toe – and zooming out, taking in a larger area of your body – your whole leg, for example. There may be parts of your body where you experience pain – of course, adjust your position accordingly but the idea is just to notice. There may be parts of your body where you can't notice any sensations – it's fine, just noticing that's the case. You might get as far as your head in the five minutes or you might find you've only explored a small area, it really doesn't matter. If your attention is wandering, and you are noticing this, patting yourself on the back for noticing! And gently bringing it back.

- **Step 3**
  When your time is up (or you're ready), bringing the exercise to a close and having a stretch.

---

Our emotions play a much bigger role in the workplace than was previously thought, evidenced by a marked increase in those seeking help for mental health issues relating to stress, anxiety and depression.[11] It no longer makes sense to seek to 'leave our emotions at the door' when we go to work. Liz Fosslien and Mollie Duffy's book *No Hard Feelings* is a great resource for navigating the workplace's emotional minefield.[12]

Although there's still widespread resistance to addressing emotions at work, this is changing with more organizations taking on board the importance of emotional literacy in boosting performance, particularly in times of transition and crisis. Emotions mobilize energy, offer important feedback in any system, help us create meaning, support decision making, and enhance relationships. Failing to acknowledge employees' emotions can hinder change programmes because people who don't feel heard often become resistant. Working well with emotions is key to excellent coaching.

In her theory Broaden and Build,[13,14] Barbara Frederickson explains that emotions such as love, joy and trust are evolved adaptations that help us build lasting resources, broadening our awareness of our surroundings and our repertoire of thoughts and actions, and helping us develop more creative, integrative, generative, curious and flexible thinking. And they boost our well-being and resilience too, building our capacity to:

- adapt to changing environments
- identify opportunities
- adapt to constraints, and
- bounce back from misfortune.

Research shows that feeling psychologically safe,[15] and thus able to trust others, helps us be successful, more creative, innovative and more collaborative – all of which are welcome in coaching.

To understand what makes teams effective and successful, Google studied 180 of its teams over two years, carrying out more than 200 interviews and analysing more than 250 different team attributes. What emerged is that the best indicator of a team's success or effectiveness was how well the team worked together and communicated, and that the most important factor was 'psychological safety'. If team members felt safe, they were:

- stronger team members
- open to diverse ideas, and
- more likely to remain with the company.

# Mind modes

Our brain has a number of modes, including *being* mode and *doing* mode. Understanding these and helping those we coach become more able to choose which to operate from can help boost performance, productivity and resilience.

Our habitual mode is doing. It's often our ally, helping us get all sorts of tasks done. But it can become our enemy. When we're stressed we tend to overuse the doing mode – worrying, analysing and problem solving. We habitually and unhelpfully turn to this mode to free ourselves from unwanted emotion, often leading to depression and anxiety. Whenever there is a sense of 'have to', 'must', 'should', 'ought' or 'need to', we can suspect the presence of doing mode.

## The discrepancy-based monitor

In Table 1, you'll see that doing mode is triggered by the discrepancy-based monitor. This is when we create an idea of how we want things to be or think they should be, and then compare that to how they are now. If there's a discrepancy, we generate thoughts and actions to try to close the gap and keep monitoring our progress; adjusting, analysing and checking accordingly. This is a system our brain has evolved over time to help us achieve many of our goals. However, it's not helpful when we apply this approach to tasks such as solving 'difficult' emotions. Zindel Segal calls problematic applications such as this 'driven-doing'.[16] We can end up over-thinking and ultimately becoming mentally and physically unwell.

| Table 1: Characteristics of Being and Doing Mind Modes

| Doing mode | Being mode |
|---|---|
| Automatic pilot | Conscious choice |
| Thinking and analysing | Sensing |
| Striving, driven, goal oriented, 'busy being busy' | Accepting, letting be and letting go |
| Seeing thoughts as solid and real | Seeing thoughts as mental events |
| Avoidance system | Approach system |
| Mental 'time travel' into the past and future | Remaining in the present moment |
| Depleting activities | Nourishing activities |
| Sympathetic nervous system dominance (fight, flight, freeze) | Parasympathetic nervous system dominance (rest and digest) |
| Triggered by the discrepancy-based monitor | |
| 'Must, have to, ought to, should...' | |

## Approach or avoid

The approach system, also known as the Behavioural Activation System, is associated with going towards, with reward, motivation and positive emotions such as hope.

The avoidance system, also known as the Behavioural Inhibition System, is associated with turning away, with avoiding things such as threat, boredom and punishment.

In coaching, we want to activate the approach system. The benefits of doing this include:

- increased well-being and resilience
- greater creativity,[17] and
- becoming better at responding rather than reacting.

This means we avoid unnecessary conflict at work and find it easier to connect with others.

We activate the approach system in Conscious Coaching through incorporating mindfulness and compassion, through the language we use (open, curious, inspiring) and how we relate to those we coach (trustworthy, warm, encouraging). In the case of unpleasant emotions, turning mindfully towards them is very often more fruitful than rejecting or suppressing them, so although they may be unwanted feelings, we're still engaging the approach system. We will explore this more in the next part, where we will learn some practical exercises to rebalance our mind modes.

# PART TWO

Making It Happen

# 4  Starting From the Inside Out: Coaching Ourselves

Having explored some of the benefits coaching, mindfulness and compassion could bring to the workplace and started to get a feel of what that might look like, we now look at how to use Conscious Coaching strategies to make the changes you want to see in yourself, your team and your organization.

Conscious Coaching is an inside-out practice, starting with our inner journey where we build self-awareness and change our own habits and way of being by:

- finding a coach
- starting to self-coach, and
- learning how to practise mindfulness and develop compassion.

## Working with a coach and a mindfulness teacher

I recommend getting a personal coach, and your own mindfulness teacher (either working one-to-one or within a group, which can be more transformative). See Appendix 1 at the back of the book for tips on picking a coach and mindfulness teacher.

## Self-coaching

What do we mean by self-coaching? It's the art of empowering ourselves through the use of coaching techniques.

Leadership coach Rachel Ellison MBE, who carried out in-depth research on self-coaching, defines it as: 'The conscious decision and ability of a leader to reflect and ask themselves coaching questions – including questions they would rather not be asked – in order to rise to a leadership challenge or think through a vision . . . You might call it self-talk or a conversation with yourself; a conscious inner dialogue, self-empowerment or the capacity to self-manage thoughts and feelings.'[1]

As we proceed, you'll get lots of ideas you can use to coach yourself, including powerful questions, models and exercises you can use for yourself as well as with others. The core principles and skills we look at for coaching also apply to self-coaching, apart from those that apply to our relationship with others. Although even aspects of those apply – we can be very harsh on ourselves, and developing a kindly approach helps us be more resourceful.

---

## Try this: Self-coaching moment

**5 Minutes**

*You will need a notebook for this exercise*

- **Step 1**
  Think of something minor that you want to address. It might be a meeting that you'd like to improve or a minor dispute between colleagues.

- **Step 2**
  Use the practice outlined on page 8, 'Getting mindful', to get into an intentioned mindset for the exercise.
- **Step 3**
  Ask yourself the following questions, reflecting between each.
  - What would be a wonderful outcome?
  - What has worked before when I've done something similar?
  - What one single step could I take now to work towards this outcome?
- **Step 4**
  Capture your reflections in a journal.

Asking ourselves the right question at the right time in just one coaching moment – or a series of questions as we press pause, get mindful and reflect – can be immensely powerful, just as it can be with others.

# 5 Coaching One-to-One: Laying the Foundations

In the next three chapters, you'll learn some important how-tos. We'll start with how to lay the foundations of a coaching relationship:

- adopting a Conscious Coaching mindset
- meeting ethical, legal and professional guidelines
- establishing an agreement.

## Adopting a Conscious Coaching mindset

As part of the philosophy underpinning Conscious Coaching, there are a number of attitudes to work towards adopting, which include those set out as attitudinal foundations for mindfulness by Jon Kabat-Zinn.[1]

As you'll see, the attitudes are interconnected, interweaving and feeding into one other. We should remember that they're aspirational and it may not be possible to embody them at all times. We might like to think of them as seeds we plant and water, in the hope that they'll grow into a beautiful, strong plant or tree representing a way of being that feeds whatever we do, including how we lead and manage others, our coaching and mindfulness practice, and the organizational culture we contribute to.

## Core attitudes of Conscious Coaching

- Beginner's mind: curiosity and openness
- Growth mindset
- Non-judging
- Letting go/be/in
- Trust
- Patience
- Acceptance
- Non-striving
- Gratitude and appreciation
- Generosity, kindness and compassion
- Courage and turning towards difficulty
- Authenticity and integrity

### Beginner's mind

> 'In the beginner's mind there are many possibilities,
> but in the expert's there are few.'
> – Shunryu Suzuki, Zen Buddhist monk[2]

If we approach each moment, situation and person as fresh and new – be that in our mindfulness practice, our coaching conversations, our dialogue as leaders, or our lives in general – we see with new eyes. By engaging the beginner's mind, we are open and curious, and as free of baggage and preconceptions as possible.[3]

### Growth mindset

In coaching, we're committed to helping ourselves and others access and harness potential, to growth and development, to working where possible from a 'growth mindset', a term coined by Carol Dweck.[4] People with a growth mindset believe they can improve and keep learning. Setbacks and challenges are perceived not as failures but as chances to keep growing and developing. Sometimes people talk about an AFLO (Another F*****g Learning Opportunity), which often makes me chuckle. Growth and learning aren't easy! Courage is required, and letting go of a desire to be perfect.

## Non-judging

This is a very important element in both mindfulness and coaching. But it's impossible to pull off non-judging completely. As human beings, we're immersed in a steady stream of judging, evaluating, coming up with an opinion – it's how our minds work.

Mindfulness teacher and Zen monk Thich Nhat Hanh talks about us all having 'inferiority, equality and superiority complexes' – we measure ourselves up against others.

The trouble is, we easily become imprisoned by our views and assumptions. We end up shutting down to different possibilities for ourselves and for others. We find it hard to be kind and compassionate to others, and thus to ourselves too, because our inner critic deafens us with judgements. In the workplace, we stamp out creativity when we rapidly judge people, their views and their actions as 'wrong' in some way.

In mindfulness, we're encouraged to actively cultivate discernment and understanding, to quieten the chatter, the constant efforts to categorize and label. It does get easier with practice. Cultivating compassion and empathy helps too – if we really 'see' and care about the other person, we're less likely to judge them negatively.

## Letting go/be/in

We easily cling to things or ideas. In coaching, we explore what is still working for us and what's no longer working for us, so we can let go of the latter.

# Try this: Letting go

**5 Minutes**

- **Step 1**
  Use the practice outlined on page 8, 'Getting mindful', to get into an intentioned mindset for the exercise.
- **Step 2**
  Taking at least three deep conscious breaths, and on each out-breath, say to yourself, 'letting go', having a sense not only of the breath leaving your body, but of letting go physically, of tension, of 'negative' emotions. Letting go into the earth.

## Trust

In both mindfulness and coaching, we seek to cultivate a sense of trust – in ourselves and in others – that we are each the best authority on ourselves and that we have inner wisdom. We trust the tried-and-tested processes of both mindfulness and coaching. Creating an atmosphere of trust in our relationships breeds psychological safety and helps us open up to change and progress.

## Patience

Impatience shows up in our body, such as holding muscular tension, and in how we present ourselves to other people – by getting angry or stressed. We miss important details and risk communication breakdowns and conflict. In the workplace, patience is an important quality, particularly when seeking to change culture. Next time you notice you're getting impatient, try the exercise below.

## Try this: Working with impatience

**5 Minutes**

**Objectives**

- Building self-awareness, particularly around what makes us lose our patience, and how this shows up in our bodies
- Building our ability to self-manage when we're 'triggered'
- Building opportunities to develop more useful strategies and beliefs

- **Step 1**
  Use the practice outlined on page 8, 'Getting mindful', to get into an intentioned mindset for the exercise.
- **Step 2**
  What are you noticing in terms of bodily sensations? Without seeking to change anything.
- **Step 3**
  Now take some deep breaths from your stomach, consciously expanding this area as you breathe in.
- **Step 4**
  Ask yourself, 'Is there a story I'm holding on to here that's unhelpful in terms of my ability to be patient?'

## Acceptance

> 'Change occurs when one becomes what he is,
> not when he tries to become what he is not.'
> – Arnold Beisser, psychiatrist and
> author, 1970[5]

The concept of acceptance can be tricky when we first come to it. We might think, 'Why would I bother with coaching if I just want to accept how things are? I want things to change!' Another word here is acknowledgement. It's about recognizing that things are how they are, that they're not always how we want them to be. This doesn't mean that we can't work to change things.

If we observe that things are how they are, we have more potential to apply wisdom. Sometimes we really can't change things but we can shift our own relationship to whatever is here. As we become more aware, we can see that struggling against whatever is here adds to our suffering.

In Buddhist teachings, the concept of the 'two arrows' describes acceptance. The first arrow is the challenge and the second arrow is how we react. Buddhists teach that we don't need the second arrow, it just adds another layer of suffering for us. Counter-intuitive though it may feel for some, the more accepting we are of our challenges, the more likely we are to be able to change them.

In Gestalt therapy and coaching, there's the idea that acceptance precedes change.[6] Gestalt's theory of change is based on the apparently paradoxical premise that people change by becoming more fully themselves, not by trying to make themselves be something or someone they are not.

## Non-striving

Non-striving is closely related to acceptance. It's about leaving behind 'driven-doing', which we looked at in Part One.

In a business environment, quite rightly, there's a strong emphasis on getting things done. On demonstrating return on investment as measured by output. As leaders and managers, we're measured by results.

Traditionally, coaching has focused on the need to strive to achieve by identifying and reaching goals. But increasingly, coaching embraces focusing on *being* as well as on *doing* and on the present (and the past) as well as the future.

Those new to mindfulness can worry that if they start practising, they'll become too relaxed and unfocused and they won't hit their targets. However, having a mindfulness practice nourishes us, so we have more energy to do more. It helps us be more productive.

In the contemporary workplace, being busy can be a badge of honour and we can feel important and useful if we're achieving. But arguably, the longer our to-do list, the more we should practice mindfulness, the more we should choose to operate from being mode so we don't get depleted. Practising mindfulness puts us more in touch with what we truly care about, and we're better able to prioritize.

But at times, we keep busy so as not to face up to ourselves – we've all had times when we're struggling and we choose to do something so we don't have to think about it. Which is fine, as long as we don't always choose that option. As we see with the ubiquitousness of presenteeism, often our doing comes from wanting to impress others, and we're not really doing as much as we seem to. Or we're doing way too much because underneath we fear being cast out. In either case, we won't increase our self-awareness by working ourselves to burnout.

# Try this: Just being

**5 Minutes**

**Objective**

- Finding opportunities to come into the present moment in our daily lives

- **Step 1**
  Use the practice outlined on page 8, 'Getting mindful', to get into an intentioned mindset for the exercise.
- **Step 2**
  Whilst you're doing something – washing up, reading this book or brushing your teeth – carrying on doing it but seeking to be more present, focusing solely on whatever you're doing.
- **Step 3**
  Trying not to get carried away by thoughts, letting yourself be immersed in the moment-to-moment experience. Just being.

## Gratitude and appreciation

> *'The butterfly counts not months but moments and has time enough.'*
> – Rabindranath Tagore, Bengali poet and musician (1861–1941)

Gratitude has been getting a lot of attention as another aspect of positive psychology. Actively focusing on what we're grateful for helps to counterbalance our natural tendency to focus on negative thought patterns.

Research highlights that developing and expressing gratitude boosts our sense of well-being and we're less likely to be depressed.[7] Gratitude strengthens interpersonal relationships, as giving thanks to others helps us form and maintain relationships, and strengthens connection and satisfaction.[8,9]

We can all think of toxic cultures, past and present, where we never seem to get thanked or appreciated, yet people are quick to jump down our throats when we do the slightest thing wrong. And yes, we can think of plenty of times when we did just that to others.

In coaching and leadership, showing appreciation helps create trust and openness. We can always find something to appreciate.

## Try this: Appreciation reflection

### 5 Minutes

- **Step 1**
  Use the practice outlined on page 8, 'Getting mindful', to get into an intentioned mindset for the exercise.
- **Step 2**
  Reflect on the following:
  - What do you appreciate about yourself?
  - What are your strengths? Your achievements? Your good qualities?
  - What do you appreciate about others (both at and outside of work)?

– How can you show appreciation, including for colleagues? (You could put in place an initiative in the organization to celebrate Employee Appreciation Day.)

## Generosity, kindness and compassion

*'Hands that give also receive.'*
– Ecuadorian proverb[10]

The Dalai Lama talks about 'enlightened self-interest' – the idea that being kind to others is a way of being kind to ourselves, as we're all interconnected.

Generosity, kindness and compassion are at the heart of mindfulness, helping us to stop being so harsh on ourselves and others. Increased compassion for self and others tends to naturally develop from practising mindfulness, but we can also actively seek to develop it.

## Courage and turning towards difficulty

In a world marked by volatility, complexity and unpredictability, we're bound at times to be confused and afraid. These times are traumatic, and I don't use the word lightly. We have to build up our courage, individually and collectively.

Being honest about that, with ourselves and others, and encouraging others to acknowledge these feelings, is healthy.

Turning inwards in mindfulness practice and in coaching to face ourselves requires patience and bravery.

Sometimes being courageous is about allowing ourselves to be vulnerable. Research professor Brené Brown is a well-known champion of vulnerability as an expression of courage. She writes: 'Our willingness to own and engage with our vulnerability determines the depth of our courage and the clarity of our purpose; the level to which we protect ourselves from being vulnerable is a measure of our fear and disconnection.'[11]

## Authenticity and integrity

> 'Beware of the man who laughs and his belly does
> not jiggle, that is a dangerous person.'
> – Confucius (551–479 BC)

We often hear about authentic leadership, and coaches frequently talk about helping clients to be their authentic selves. It can sometimes feel like a hollow word, but it's key in emotional intelligence. Authenticity is about knowing what our values are, being able to articulate these, and ensuring our behaviours are congruent with them. Integrity involves being ethical and trustworthy.

## Conscious Coaching competencies

Conscious Coaching is built on the core coaching competencies set out by leading professional coaching bodies, including the International Coach Federation, Association for Coaching and the European Mentoring and Coaching Council. What makes Conscious Coaching different to some other styles of coaching is that it specifically draws on mindfulness and compassion, to enable and enhance the development of these competencies.

Table 2 summarizes the core competencies of Conscious Coaching.

| Table 2: Core Conscious Coaching Competencies

> **Putting in place the right foundation:**
> - Meeting ethical, legal and professional guidelines
> - Establishing the coaching agreement and outcomes
>
> **Co-creating the right kind of relationship:**
> - Establishing trust, psychological safety and intimacy
> - Managing self and maintaining presence
>
> **Communicating effectively:**
> - Deep active listening
> - Powerful questioning and use of silence
> - Direct communication
>
> **Facilitating learning and results:**
> - Adopting a facilitative, non-directive stance
> - Encouraging accountability
> - Raising awareness and insight
> - Designing strategies and actions
> - Maintaining forward momentum and evaluation

## Meeting ethical, legal and professional guidelines

This includes:

- understanding and being able to communicate the differences between coaching and other support interventions
- having duty of care to others and pointing them, where necessary, to other professionals if they need a different kind of support (for example, to an Employee Assistance Programme, or notifying HR)
- being guided by a clear code of ethics.[12]

## Establishing an agreement

In formal, professional workplace coaching, a contract is often agreed between the person being coached, their manager and the coach.

If you're planning a more casual coaching style, sometimes referred to as 'corridor coaching', you won't need to agree a formal contract before starting but even for a one-off one-to-one coaching session with someone, it can be helpful to agree a contract for working together.

Here are some questions to explore when thinking about or drawing up the agreement.

- **How do we want to work together?**
  What will the coaching consist of? What's the approach? (For example, having a conversation or series of conversations to help you find your own answers.) How many sessions? What if the other person seems to need support from a qualified professional such as a therapist? What if the relationship isn't working, or the coaching isn't going anywhere?

- **What do we want to work on?**
  What's the overarching purpose or intention for the coaching?

In Appendix 2, you'll find responses to some frequently asked questions to help you plan your coaching.

# 6 Coaching One-to-One: Building Rapport

The relationship is king in coaching. According to Erik de Haan, director of the Ashridge Centre for Coaching, the coaching relationship is the 'only genuinely effective ingredient we are able to influence'.[1] The strength and nature of the relationship between coaches and executives is a critical success factor in successful coaching outcomes.[2]

In this chapter you'll learn:

- how to get started with the person you're coaching (your 'coachee'):
  - co-creating the coaching relationship
  - communication techniques:
    - deep listening
    - clarifying and reflecting
    - powerful questioning
    - the use of silence
    - facilitating learning
  - working with stories.

## Co-creating and taking care of the relationship

Drawing on mindfulness and compassion can help enormously to build a strong relationship, creating rapport and trust, and thus the right conditions for great coaching outcomes. A big part of establishing trust is being able to tune into others and demonstrate care and concern for others. Research on cognitive behavioural interventions suggests that 'empathic curiosity' – the ability to listen and engage with the person being coached with an open and curious attitude, asking the right questions and building rapport – improves the outcome for them.[3]

### How to build rapport with a new coachee

Starting each conversation with a mindfulness practice can be very powerful, helping to create deep rapport and empathy.

## Try this: Connecting through mindfulness

**5 Minutes**

- **Step 1**
  Use the practice outlined on page 8, 'Getting mindful', to get into an intentioned mindset for the exercise.
- **Step 2**
  Once you're with the person, *invite* them to join you in your mindfulness practice so they don't feel uncomfortable, suggesting they close their eyes or gaze downwards, feeling their feet on the floor, taking three deep conscious breaths, 'letting go' on the out-breath.

I stress 'invite' because not everyone will be receptive, but I find most people are, particularly if we frame it as getting more grounded to enable a better quality conversation.

We may experience a natural rapport in our coaching relationship because we feel the other person is similar to us in the way they look, dress, their cultural background, how they speak, their values and so on.

When there's rapport, there's likely to be matching or 'mimicking' in all sorts of areas between you and the other person, including posture, gestures, breathing, volume, speed and energy of speech. This can happen without us being aware of it.

One study found that cortisol levels increased in people who weren't being 'mimicked' (where there weren't signs of matching). Non-mimicking can make us feel we're being socially excluded, which is stressful for most people.[4]

In coaching we actively seek to be aware of the process and work with it to increase rapport. Drawing on mindfulness techniques helps us be more conscious of what's happening in our own field of awareness, including verbal and non-verbal body language.

### Signs of a lack of rapport

- Feeling a lack of warmth and openness from the other person
- The other person looking away and fidgeting
- You feeling restless and uncomfortable or a sense of detachment or separation
- The other person suddenly slumping while you're sitting upright

- You're speaking quickly while they're speaking slowly
- They're speaking quietly but you're speaking loudly

So what can you do when you notice any of the above? If you notice a sudden break in rapport, this can be because something has come up in the person's exploration. For example, they might feel overwhelmed about the issue.

Approach the problem by sharing what you noticed. 'I noticed that as you were talking about that particular project, your energy seemed to dip. Can you say anything about that?'

Or they might suddenly start speeding up in their speech. They might sound agitated, and you might say, 'As you talk about working with the new team, you seemed to be more agitated. I was wondering what was going on for you there?'

Or perhaps they're excited, and you might feed back, 'You really seem energized as you describe your vision for the department.'

If there really isn't any rapport, and you can't seem to build it, name it. It happens. You could suggest reviewing how you're getting on as a matter of course: 'We've been having coaching conversations on a few occasions now, and I'm wondering how we think we're getting on, what's working for us, and what isn't working so well.'

Listen to what they say, and if nothing shifts rapport-wise, you might conclude that you've come to the end of your coaching with them and make some suggestions for others they can work with.

You can refer back to the coaching contract, particularly if you've been explicit that if it isn't working for either of you, there's a 'no-blame clause' for exiting.

## Communicating effectively

### Deep listening

When was the last time someone really listened to you? Not only without checking their mobile but with full presence, without interrupting, offering you a sense of being really heard? If it was recently, you're very lucky.

There are a number of levels of listening (Figure 2), although the lower level doesn't really count as listening.

| Figure 2: Listening Levels Bandwidth

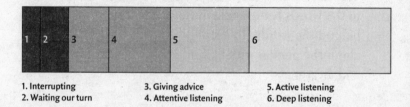

1. Interrupting          3. Giving advice          5. Active listening
2. Waiting our turn      4. Attentive listening    6. Deep listening

- **Level 1: Interrupting**

- **Level 2: Waiting our turn**
  Carol Wilson, founder of Culture at Work, calls this 'hijacking'. We're quiet, but we're just waiting for a chance to say what's in our mind, often to share a story which takes away from what others are saying. We all know how annoying it is when someone keeps doing that. But we do it ourselves more than we think.

- **Level 3: Giving advice**
  This may be entirely appropriate but we want to listen to the other person first to see what they can come up with. As managers and leaders, we jump to giving advice (and of course, it's expected) all too readily.

- **Level 4: Attentive listening**
  Here we exhibit behaviours that show we're listening; maybe our head is cocked to one side, we're looking at the speaker, we may be nodding.

- **Level 5: Active listening**
  This is coaching-level listening. In addition to listening to the words being spoken, we're listening to what's behind the words. To silences. To our intuition. It's all about the person with us, and enabling their learning and awareness.

- **Level 6: Deep listening**
  In Conscious Coaching, we add another level, what Thich Nhat Hanh calls 'deep listening' or 'compassionate listening'. We listen to what our bodies are telling us. We may have a knot in our stomach and we don't know why – we might be tapping into something to do with what the other person is experiencing. We draw on compassion development techniques, which allow us to tune into what our hearts are telling us.
  Active listening is hard work, deep listening even more so. And it's one of the best gifts we can offer one another. It's something we have to practice – and we all have plenty of opportunity to do that with those around us. Why don't you start right now?

# Try this: Deep listening

## 5 Minutes

The next person you come across, instead of being caught up totally in what you're doing and what you have to do next, make a conscious effort to listen fully.

## Objectives

- Perfecting the art of deep listening
- Accessing more information about what's being said and what's not being said
- Boosting connection with others
- Increasing the chance of the other person feeling heard and understood

- **Step 1**
  Use the practice outlined on page 8, 'Getting mindful', to get into an intentioned mindset for the exercise.
- **Step 2**
  Sitting back in your chair, or standing upright, relaxing, looking them in the eyes, seeing if you can hold the intention to just be there for them, no agenda of your own, and listening. No interrupting. No advising. Just listening deeply. It will come with practice.
- **Step 3**
  You may know them well enough and feel comfortable enough to share what you just did, and even to ask them about its impact. Feedback is very helpful as we practise more and more.

## Clarifying and reflecting

Clarifying or paraphrasing is a technique used often in coaching to help the other person feel heard and understood.

Here's an example.

The coachee says, 'I struggle to speak up in meetings, I can sometimes be about to say something but then I feel too nervous.'

You say, 'It sounds like you find it hard to be assertive.'

Reflecting means repeating back to the other person their exact words. This helps to check that you interpreted what they said correctly, and to move them forward.

Here's an example.

The coachee says, 'I don't know if I'm in the right role, although I love the team and what we're trying to achieve.'

You say, 'You don't feel like you're in the right role?'

## Powerful questioning

It's not only about listening, asking questions is a big part of coaching. We should always try to make our questions simple, clear and open. Open questions are those that cannot be answered with a yes or no. They tend to begin with *what, when, how* or *where* (avoiding *why* is advisable, as it can trigger defensiveness).

The important thing is to be led by the person and the issue. Your role is to help them find what they need, rather than tell them.

Here are some of the reasons why we ask questions in coaching.

- To help people move on when they are stuck in their thinking

- To prompt a different way of approaching something and to access hidden wisdom
- To help someone consider the bigger picture
- To identify possible solutions
- To help clarify next steps

Here are some useful questions you may like to try using in your coaching.

- What would happen if nothing changed?
- What's standing in your way?
- What has worked well for you in a similar situation in the past?
- If you DID know, what would you say?
- Who else is affected by this? What would others in your system say?
  Here we tap into the person's system. What would a friend say? A colleague? Direct reports? All the various stakeholders? What about the system itself, if it could speak? What about the natural world? Children of the future?
- What do you really care about?
  What they first say they care about isn't necessarily what they truly care about. When they come to a natural stop, you can ask, 'And what else?'
- And what else?
  This warrants its own slot. Some of our best thinking comes after the first load of stuff that comes out of our mouths, which is stuff we know already, or which we think the other person wants to hear.
- What needs to happen then?
- What ideas are coming up for you?

- What are the options you're considering?
- What are your next steps?
- How will you know when you've got there?

Below are some questions to pose when the person is stuck or needs inspiration. Perhaps they've got bogged down in describing the minutiae of a situation, and their energy is low. Pick those relevant to the particular dialogue and exploration.

- The miracle question
  Imagine you go to sleep tonight and overnight a miracle happens. When you wake up, things are exactly as you want them to be. What will they be like? What will you see, hear, feel?
- Between the ages of four and twelve, what were your favourite activities, ones during which you lost sense of time?
- What brings you joy? What brought you joy when you were little?
- In the past, when you've experienced deep insight, what were the circumstances? What can you learn from that in relation to now?
- What does your heart tell you?
- What does your body tell you?
- What are you grateful for?
- Which stories in your life are working for you?
- Which stories are not working for you?
- Which new stories do you want to create?
- What question do you want to be asked?
- What question do you NOT want to be asked?
- What are the questions that won't go away?

- Who inspires you? Who do you want to be like?
- Where do you see yourself in five years' time? What steps do you need to take to get to this point?
- How do you want to be remembered?
  Imagine it's your ninetieth birthday party and everyone is there – loved ones, work colleagues, former rivals. What are they saying about you?

In Conscious Coaching, in particular, it's important to trust the process, for all parties to get into as mindful a state as possible and just see what emerges. Don't get too hung up on asking the perfect question and don't worry if the person doesn't have anything to say in response. The best kinds of questions are those that naturally emerge from deep listening and from being unattached to a specific outcome.

## The sound of silence

Making time to be in silence can be immensely nourishing and resourcing. We can combine it with a brief mindfulness practice.

All too often we rush to fill silence, and ruin people's opportunities to come up with their own answers and insights. When those we're coaching are silent, they may be generating their best thinking. Their body language gives us clues – looking off into the distance or cocking their head to one side suggests deep thinking. To avoid awkwardness, we can say or signal to people that we're going to give them time to think.

## Establishing a facilitative style

Generally, we should communicate directly and effectively in coaching, we need to use appropriate and respectful language. We need to be clear with those we coach about the objectives for the coaching, the purpose of techniques or exercises, and when offering any feedback, with examples where possible. Key to this is establishing a facilitative style.

## Ask, don't tell

As managers and leaders, we're expected to give orders. But as we saw earlier, there's been a marked shift towards leaders being able to flex between different styles.

Adopting a facilitative non-directive style encourages and empowers the other person to think for themselves, to be self-directed. There'll be many times when you feel you have the right and best answer, and it will be painful to hold back, but you must.

There may be times when it's important or highly relevant to give advice, but we should do so very sparingly, and only as an offering or suggestion, and with permission. We might say, 'Something's coming up for me that may or may not be useful for you. May I share it with you?'

Remember, though, that if you're someone's boss, any suggestion may be heard as an order.

It can be helpful to think of a spectrum, a slider scale between directive and non-directive, as illustrated below. As a

| Figure 3: The Directive–Non-Directive Spectrum

| Directive | | Non-directive/ self-directed |
|---|---|---|
| I know | ←→ | You know |
| I have the solution | ←→ | You have |
| I tell you and you do as I say | ←→ | You choose |

leader or manager, you need to be able to slide along, back and forth, as required, and generally staying in the non-directive/self-directed space on the right when coaching.

## Reframing

One communication tool for creating awareness is reframing, which is about viewing the current situation from a different perspective, changing the meaning that's attributed. Let's explore.

Reframing helps people to:

- get 'unstuck' and gain clarity and solve problems by viewing things from alternative standpoints
- increase resilience by developing strategies such as seeing negative situations as opportunities for learning and growth.

Try using some of these questions in your coaching to prompt reframing.

- Is this the right thing to be focusing on?
- Is it the problem itself or how you view it?
- What might be a different way of viewing this? What might a colleague or friend say?
- How can we shift the focus, from, for example, you to others / past to future / victimhood to empowerment / negative to positive / passive to active / impossible to possible?
- What learning opportunities might be present as a result of this situation?

In Conscious Coaching, we not only encourage reframing through traditional methods, such as questioning assumptions and exploring blind spots in dialogue, we do so through mindfulness, including silent meditation practice.

Reframing can come through changing our relationship with our thoughts. The more we practise in mindfulness meditation noticing our thoughts, the more we realize not only how easy it is to get carried away on a train of thought, but also that thoughts are self-generating, that we're not driving the thinking – thoughts just pop up. We realize we don't have to identify with every thought and that thoughts don't have to define who we are. We are not our thoughts. By creating more distance between 'us' and our thoughts, we gain more choice as to whether we engage, as to whether we 'get on the train' or not.

## Try this: Mindfulness of thoughts

### 5 Minutes

### Objectives

- Becoming more self-aware
- Coming to realize thoughts aren't facts
- Gaining choice over which thoughts to engage with

- **Step 1**
  Use the practice outlined on page 8, 'Getting mindful', to get into an intentioned mindset for the exercise.
- **Step 2**
  Tuning into the sounds around you. Having a sense of sounds coming and going, like events, with a beginning, a middle and an end. Imagining you're like a radio tuned into a particular station, just receiving the sounds without having to do anything, including interpreting the sounds.

- **Step 3**
  Switching your focus to your thoughts. Just like
  you did with sounds, imagining you're 'watching'
  or receiving the thoughts. Just like the sounds,
  they're coming and going. A common metaphor
  is that of thoughts being like clouds passing through
  the sky. If you find you've jumped on a train of
  thoughts, don't worry, just noticing that's happened,
  and gently bringing your attention back to the
  thoughts.

## Working with stories

Paying attention to language is important too – words have power. Changing the language we use can help us to reframe our situation. One way to do this is to look at the stories we tell ourselves, and others.

In recent years we've seen more than ever before the power of stories, for good and bad, just look at the spread of fake news in the political landscape. Stories can be very damaging but they can also be very healing – 'medicine', as Jungian analyst and poet Clarissa Estés describes them.[5]

In innovative Japanese internet company Ozvision,[6] employees gather in their teams each morning for a meeting called 'good or new'. Employees take it in turns to share something, which doesn't have to be work-related. Another storytelling practice they engage in seeks to foster gratitude. Each employee can take an additional day off every year, called a 'day of thanking', and each receives $200 to use to thank someone special. The deal is that they have to then share with colleagues the story of what they gave and how it landed.

In coaching, we can harness the power of storytelling in a number of ways.

---

## Try this: Lifeline exercise

**30 Minutes**

**Objectives**

- Identifying:
  - patterns and themes in our lives and careers, in our beliefs and behaviours
  - areas for further development, and strengths and passions
  - solutions and techniques that have worked in the past

- **Step 1**
  Use the practice outlined on page 8, 'Getting mindful', to get into an intentioned mindset for the exercise.
- **Step 2**
  Invite others to reflect on their life/career up until this point, and to draw their 'lifeline' or 'career line', marking significant moments including 'highs' and 'lows'.
- **Step 3**
  Use the coaching conversation to explore what has emerged.

---

Here are some questions to explore in the lifeline exercise.

- What are the common themes and patterns in the story of your life?

- Who has been important in your life and why?
- What have been your most meaningful moments in your life/work, and why?
- What do these tell you about how you respond and react?
- What can you learn about what has worked well and what not so well?
- What can you learn about your strengths and weaknesses?
- Which are the stories we regularly tell ourselves about who we are and why we do what we do?
- Do they still serve us or do we need new stories? If so, what are these?

Here are some other questions to explore more generally around stories.

- Which were your favourite childhood stories?
- Which characters were you drawn to, or repelled by?
- Do you find yourself expressing any of their qualities at work? What does doing so mean for those around you?

# 7 One-to-One Coaching: Facilitating Learning and Results

Coaching in the workplace is all about facilitating learning and results. If that isn't happening, it's not effective coaching. We've already looked at some ways to facilitate learning in the previous chapter. In this chapter we'll focus on how to facilitate learning and results through:

- goal setting
- recording progress
- approaching obstacles.

We'll start with a tool which creates awareness and helps the coachee learn in a mindful, compassionate way.

## The FELT model

The FELT model[1] is one that I've developed for use in self-coaching, one-to-one coaching conversations, or in team/group coaching and gatherings to mindfully explore:

- a particular question or issue
- emotions that you sense are there but haven't unpacked, or difficult emotions that you/others are aware of

- what the body has to tell us, including around stress management and well-being, or what's going on in a relationship
- what a new mindset, way of being, vision or strategy might be like
- when problem solving isn't working (by promoting direct experience, it allows access to a different kind of knowing).

FELT incorporates a number of key components of mindfulness, including:

- attention to the present moment
- attentional control (the practice of intentionally directing our attention to a chosen object, noticing when our attention wanders, bringing it back and building capacity to maintain focus)
- curiosity and enquiry
- kindness and compassion (towards self and others)
- non-judgement
- acceptance
- letting go/be/in

You can choose to move through the model in a linear fashion or stay within one or two parts of the model – spending a whole session 'exploring', or working with 'letting go, letting be, letting in'.

The power of the model is that it helps us to stay in mindful enquiry, in direct experience or being mode, and not get caught up in over-thinking. If you find your mind is wandering off and interpreting, you can gently guide yourself back to noticing bodily sensations.

# Try this: The FELT model

If you're doing it for yourself, you might want to record yourself reading through the text, so you don't have to keep referring back. To make it easier to use with others, I've put text you can use as a script in italics and marked where to pause. You can give them two options.

1 To be led through the process without having to respond out loud. You can then debrief afterwards.
2 To respond as you lead them through the process.

- **Step 1**
  Use the practice outlined on page 8, 'Getting mindful', to get into an intentioned mindset for the exercise.
  *To help you stay internally focused, closing your eyes or gazing downwards. Feeling your feet on the floor, bringing your attention to your breathing and noticing any bodily sensations that are present as you breathe.*
- **Step 2: Setting the intention**
  *In addition to choosing the topic, setting intentions to be curious and open, parking any assumptions and the temptation to interpret, to be kind and compassionate towards yourself as best you can.*
  PAUSE . . .
- **Step 3: Exploring the topic**
  *Exploring what's showing up around your topic (which may shift as you proceed). Remembering to explore with self-compassion and kindliness, curiosity and non-judgement. Just being open to whatever arises.*

## PAUSE . . .

*I'm now going to ask you some potentially catalytic questions to help you continue to explore mindfully. Spend time with each question that you're drawn to, and ignore any that don't resonate.*

If you're leading a coachee through the exercise, explain these questions are invitational, and make sure you pause between asking each.

- *What is wanting to be noticed?*
- *Are you noticing any bodily sensations? If so, where, and are they static or shifting and morphing?*
- *Does whatever is present have a name or names?*
- *A colour or colours?*
- *A shape or shapes?*
- *What is whatever is present asking for? What does it want or need?*
- *Is there any wisdom from your body that is making itself known, telling you something you didn't know?*
- *Are there any feelings that are coming up?*

*Whatever is coming up, sitting with it, not grasping after it, nor turning away from it. If something feels a bit tricky, 'cradling' it, 'embracing' it gently, with non-judgement and compassion or kindness, giving it space.*

Buddhist monk Thich Nhat Hanh suggests having in mind the image of gently cradling a baby when difficult emotions arise. If anger arises, we turn towards and lightly embrace the anger, rather than giving in to the desire to push it away, or evaluate and criticize.

We're playing around with acceptance. We might label whatever it is, thus creating some distance.

*If at any time you're finding the exploration overly intense, coming back to your breath if that works for you as an anchor, or to bodily sensations.*

- **Step 4: Letting go, letting be, letting in**
*Now exploring if there is anything that has come up that you would like to **let go** of, such as something that no longer serves you.*
PAUSE . . .
*And now, exploring whether there's anything that's calling to be let alone, to be **let be**, to stay as it is, for now at least.*
PAUSE . . .
*Finally, considering if there is anything you want to **let in**. Maybe there's a new belief, or a 'mantra' – a phrase that sums up your insights, or new behaviour.*

- **Step 5: Transforming**
*Now sitting with all that has arisen, noticing what is going on in your body, thoughts and feelings. What, if any, wisdom is making itself known? What, if anything, is needing or wanting to transform?*

*This might involve actively changing something, a behaviour or mindset, or even a value, but all coming from a place of wisdom, of compassion, of sitting with 'not-knowing', and from 'knowing' as opposed to knowledge in the form of information. This step can be about taking time to embody a shift that has arisen from the exploration. And when you're ready, opening your eyes.*

*Now taking time to capture any insights in your journal and to reflect on any next steps and goals to work with if desired.*

(Or you can now debrief in the coaching.)

# Walking

> 'Methinks that the moment my legs begin to move,
> my thoughts begin to flow.'
> – Henry David Thoreau[2]

Combining coaching with walking can be very fruitful. When we walk, the heart pumps faster, circulating more blood and oxygen to all our organs, including the brain, boosting memory and attention. We can stroll at our own pace, matching what's going on with our moods and our inner speech. Our attention is free to wander, given that we probably don't have to pay much attention to the act of walking, and we may enter a mental state conducive to innovation and insight. Walking opens up the free flow of ideas, boosting creativity both while we're walking and shortly after.[3]

Not everyone likes to sit and meditate and, if that is the case, you may enjoy moving mindfully instead. We can do any movement mindfully – running, swimming, dancing and walking. Mindful walking lends itself beautifully to supporting self or other coaching. Or you can walk mindfully to a coaching conversation or any other meeting.

## Try this: Mindful walking

**10 Minutes**

**Objectives**

- Introducing a mindful practice that can be done pretty much anywhere

- Using the body as an anchor to bring you into the present moment
- Working with movement as a way to become mindful, which some people prefer to sitting still

- **Step 1**
  Use the practice outlined on page 8, 'Getting mindful', to get into an intentioned mindset for the exercise.
- **Step 2**
  Paying close attention to the ordinary action of walking, becoming aware of the movements associated with each step you take, noticing sensations in your body as you lift each foot and place it down, sensations in your feet, your ankles, your legs, your back, your shoulders. It's easier if you do it slowly, but you don't have to. Playing around with coordinating your breathing with each step.

## Location, location, location

In addition to simply walking mindfully, and then seeing what comes up, we can work creatively with context and setting. Below are some suggestions for things to try, to help create awareness, prompting new thinking and different perspectives. Keep a notebook handy in which you and whoever you coach can capture what comes up.

# Try this: Location coaching

- **Step 1**
  Choose your location and setting.
- **Step 2**
  Use the practice outlined on page 8, 'Getting mindful', to get into an intentioned mindset for the exercise.
- **Step 3: Exploring your Triangle of Awareness**
  How is your body feeling? How are your feet making contact with the floor?

  Then, breathing normally, but becoming aware of what's going on in your body as you breathe in and out – your abdomen rising and falling. Is there anything your body is telling you? Which, if any, feelings do you notice? Where are you noticing those in your body, if you are? Your thoughts: are you aware of any thoughts in particular coming in?
- **Step 4: Mindful walking**
  Starting to walk around mindfully. At this stage, you're focusing on the walking itself, as outlined in the mindful walking practice above.
- **Step 5: Mindful exploration**
  Now, with your chosen topic accompanying you, taking in your environment. While you are wandering about, noticing what you're drawn to. What's leaving you cold? What's repelling, angering, irritating you? What's showing up in your Triangle of Awareness as you explore? What's your heart telling you? Keeping exploring mindfully: what else are you noticing?

When you're ready, capturing what's come up in your notebook. Do you notice any patterns? Any insights in relation to your chosen topic?

- **Step 6: Optional 'powerful questions'**
  If you fancy, playing around with some of the questions I suggested earlier.

## Nature

Being out in nature boosts creative problem solving, partly because exposure to nature arouses positive emotions and also because, in doing so, we're spending less time on attention-demanding technology.[4]

Spending time in nature can form part of our self-care regime. A study on people suffering from depression found those who walked in nature experienced more of an improvement in their moods, as well as their memory span, compared to those walking in an urban setting.[5] Exercise generally has been shown to improve mood, but it seems that 'green exercise' in particular helps to reduces anxiety.[6] People with mental health issues found that engaging in exercise in nature brought significant improvements in self-esteem and mood levels.[7] Getting out into nature helps to restore mental well-being through alleviating stress and anxiety, facilitating emotional perspective, clarity and reassurance, and through the maintenance of positive family dynamics.[8]

## Urban coaching

Although spending time in an urban setting can be draining, as there is so much to take in and negotiate – whilst being in nature enables our minds to move in a relaxed way from one sensory experience to another – the urban environment can have something to offer too, apart from it sometimes being the easiest to access from the workplace.

Samsung, Cancer Research UK and Google Netherlands are among a growing number of organizations sending employees out into the streets, taking part in events created by global social enterprise Street Wisdom. Founder David Pearl's mission is to enable 'anyone, anywhere to get unusual inspiration from their everyday surroundings', gaining skills to 'access the "invisible university" that's all around them and find fresh answers to personal or work-related questions'. If we approach town/city life with curiosity, we can indeed enhance well-being and prompt new thinking. And of course it's often what's nearest to us at work. The trick is to approach it with new eyes, with the mindful qualities I outlined earlier, including curiosity, openness and appreciation, and working with a specific process such as that outlined above.

### Culture-based coaching

Visiting art galleries with a view to doing some coaching can not only be fun but can prompt new thinking and perspectives. Say you choose an exhibition of paintings. See which painting you and/or others are drawn to. Really notice what draws you into the painting. Notice what attracts you, what calls for your attention. What about the elements that arouse 'negative' emotions? What might these reactions tell you?

You can do this with other art too – including graffiti.

And you don't have to be on the move – you can work with novels, poems, films and so on. Notice which words stand out for you? Which characters? What are they telling you? There is wisdom all around.

### Client story: María

In one coaching session, leader María explored the 'Fall of Lucifer' painting by nineteenth-century Romantic painter Antonio María Esquivel, on display at the time in the Prado gallery in Madrid. María wasn't religious but knew the story about Lucifer being one of God's favourite angels until he rebelled, and was thus cast out. The 1840 painting features a stern-faced St Michael casting out an angry-looking Lucifer.

For María, the painting prompted her to explore themes of power dynamics, her own desire for 'rebellion' at work, as she was feeling unaligned with the CEO's values, and the possible consequences of going through with 'rebellion' and what that might look like. What was best for her, and for the organization? Who did Lucifer and St Michael represent for her? She reflected that perhaps her boss was best represented by Lucifer who needed to be cast out either in the sense of him leaving the organization, or metaphorically by her not letting him have so much power over her. She explored the emotions that were aroused in her in looking at the painting: anger, for example; sadness that 'things have to be so black and white' at work sometimes; desiring 'more colour'; and grief as she was missing how things used to be with the previous CEO. We explored where the feelings and emotions showed up in her body. She noticed that she was making herself small physically, and that she had a knot in her stomach. She could then identify next steps, including taking care of her well-being.

# Try this: Future Self exercise

**15 Minutes**

**Objectives**

- Drawing on hope and optimism
- Enabling access to inner wisdom
- Identifying next steps

You may choose to read through the text, perhaps recording yourself. You can do it on your own, or with your team.

- **Step 1**
  Use the practice outlined on page 8, *Getting mindful,* to get into an intentioned mindset for the exercise.
- **Step 2**
  What is going on in your Triangle of Awareness right now: body, feelings, thoughts?
- **Step 3**
  Cast your mind to the future, 10 to 15 years from now. How and who do you want to be? You might want to take 10 to 15 steps forward. Then, having taken your steps into the future, taking some mindful breaths and tuning into your Future Self.
  Ask yourself questions such as:
  - Where am I?
  - What can I see, taste, smell, hear, touch?
  - Who am I now?
  - What are my favourite things to do?
  - What is a typical day?

- What are my values?
- What am I feeling?
- What counsel, pearls of wisdom, insight, does my Future Self wish to share with my Earlier Self?

- **Step 4**
Then, turn around and look back to where you started from. As you look back, what is coming up for you in terms of steps you'd need to take to get from there to here? Insights? What are your body and your heart telling you?

- **Step 5**
Now, take 10 to 15 steps back and, looking to the future, tune in again. What else are you noticing?

- **Step 6**
Finally, take some time to capture in your journal what's come up for you.

## Try this: Mindful multiple perspectives

### 30 Minutes

I developed this to enable the exploration of an issue through a number of lenses.

### Objectives

- Accessing a range of perspectives
- Accessing inner wisdom and intuition
- Identifying next steps

We can do it on paper. Or we can move around the room, taking different positions for each perspective – this can work really well.

- **Step 1**
  Use the practice outlined on page 8, 'Getting mindful', to get into an intentioned mindset for the exercise.
- **Step 2**
  Setting your intention and choosing your issue for the exercise.
- **Step 3**
  Go leisurely through each of the following perspectives in turn. At each stage, noticing what's coming up for you in general and in relation to your issue.
  - **Perspective 1: Present moment**
    Without over-thinking, first thoughts and impressions.
  - **Perspective 2: Body wisdom**
    Bodily sensations and messages from your body.
  - **Perspective 3: Single-pointed focus**
    Narrowing your focus as if you're shining a spotlight directly on the issue.
  - **Perspective 4: Wider focus**
    Adopting a 'helicopter view', imagining you're relaxing your eyes and tapping into your peripheral vision but still with your issue in mind.
  - **Perspective 5: Compassion**
    If we wish, placing our hands on our heart, and asking what our heart has to say about the issue.

- **Perspective 6: 'Choiceless awareness'**
  This means no longer choosing to focus on anything in particular, just resting in openness to whatever arises.
- **Step 4**
  Capture any insights in your journal.

## Try this: Art-based coaching

### 10 Minutes

This is easy to do on your own or with others. You will need some paper and pens.

### Objectives

- Getting 'unstuck'
- Having fun
- Accessing inner wisdom and intuition

- **Step 1**
  Use the practice outlined on page 8, 'Getting mindful', to get into an intentioned mindset for the exercise.
- **Step 2**
  Setting your intention for the exercise.
- **Step 3**
  Without thinking too hard, draw whatever comes up.
- **Step 4**
  Discuss and identify next steps.

## Mindful systemic constellations

The exercises below draw on work in the field of Systemic Constellations, including Bert Hellinger's in Family Constellations. Systemic Constellations is 'a method, an approach, a type of therapy, a collection of insights, applied philosophy, study of human relationships, a useful tool applied in many disciplines, a way of perceiving the world', according to the International Systemic Constellation Association.[9]

In business, constellations are typically used by leaders and managers to examine pressing issues, and to surface habitual systemic patterns or hidden dynamics in personal relationships.

Key concepts are:

- the whole is greater than the sum of its parts –
  a team or organization is more than just a number
  of individuals put together
- all elements in a system are interdependent –
  changing one element will impact all other
  elements.

## Try this: Constellations exercise

### 20–30 Minutes

In this systemic enquiry exercise, you can identify which people and elements are in the system, and what they represent, demand, offer and so on.

## Objectives

- Helping you make decisions about the company or team as a whole
- Discovering ways to solve conflict between team members

### Version 1: Using objects

- **Step 1**
  Gather a number of objects. It doesn't matter what they are, various pens and pencils would work.
- **Step 2**
  Setting your intention.
- **Step 3**
  Use the practice outlined on page 8, 'Getting mindful', to get into an intentioned mindset for the exercise.
- **Step 4**
  On a flat surface, set out the various items to represent what/who they need to represent. Don't over-think it in terms of layout – see what emerges naturally.
- **Step 5**
  Next, mindfully explore what you see and pick up. Look at things like the distance between the objects, where they are in relation to each other, the space you've taken up for the whole constellation. What are the objects telling you? Are there any needs they're expressing, perhaps ones you weren't aware of?
- **Step 6**
  What are your thoughts, feelings and body telling you?
- **Step 7**
  Close your eyes and take some mindful breaths.

- **Step 8**
  Open them and look again at the constellation.
  What are the patterns? What do you need to listen
  to? Anything need to shift? What might be a better
  position? What actions are required?

**Version 2: Drawing**
Follow the same steps as above. But instead of using
objects, draw out the constellation.

## Designing actions and strategies

Goal setting and planning is a key area when it comes to designing actions. We do this in every session. It helps to encourage accountability, and maintain forward momentum and
evaluation.

Goal setting has been pivotal in traditional coaching. It's
the first stage of one of the most commonly known coaching
framework models, the GROW model, popularized by one of
business coaching's forefathers, the late Sir John Whitmore.[10]

### The GROW framework
GROW has been used successfully for many years as a framework for both informal coaching-style conversations and more
formal coaching sessions, in self-coaching, individual and
team/group coaching, or in a team meeting. It's simple, and
accessible, particularly to those new to coaching.

- **Goal setting:** for a particular coaching conversation/
  session as well as in the short and long term

- **R**eality: exploring the current situation
- **O**ptions and alternative strategies or courses of action
- **W**hat is to be done, **W**hen, by **W**hom, and the **W**ill to do it

## The EXACT framework

Leaders I work with find the model EXACT, developed by Carol Wilson, founder of Culture at Work, useful as a goal-setting framework, identifying goals that are congruent with the person's own values and performance style, rather than being determined by the agenda or pressure of others.

- **E**xplicit (succinct and one focus)
- e**X**citing (positively framed and inspiring)
- **A**ssessable (measurable)
- **C**hallenging (stretching)
- **T**ime-framed (preferably within three to six months)

While goal setting is useful in coaching, in Conscious Coaching there isn't such an attachment to this for a number of reasons. One is that in these unpredictable complex times, it's often impossible to start with a clear idea of where we'll end up. Another is that goals often naturally shift as we move through a series of coaching conversations, or even in the first chat, and new information and wisdom emerges. The last reason is that when we embrace mindfulness principles, we'll appreciate that holding on too tightly to a goal can actually hinder what could be a highly fruitful emergent process.

It can be more helpful to frame and explore what our overarching purpose or intention is, which is what we do in my model below.

# Try this: The 'four-eyed' model

## 20 Minutes

### Objectives

- Offering an alternative framework to explore and identify next steps when there's a sense that it's not going to be easy, relevant or helpful to zoom in on specific goals – at this stage at least
- Allowing lots of space for things to emerge whilst avoiding meandering and still making clear progress

- **Step 1**
  Use the practice outlined on page 8, 'Getting mindful', to get into an intentioned mindset for the exercise.
- **Step 2**
  Intention
  - What do you want to explore? What is the overarching purpose of having this conversation?
- **Step 3**
  Ideas: brainstorm
  - Which ideas are coming up for you?
- **Step 4**
  Inspiration
  - Which of these actually inspire you?
- **Step 5**
  Initiation
  - To get started, what do you need to do, how do you want to do it . . . etc? Where can you look? Who can you ask?

## Uncovering and working with bias and judgement

We naturally judge others, as we've seen, and we all hold unconscious biases.

The potential of mindfulness for addressing and challenging unconscious bias in the workplace has been highlighted by lots of researchers. Practising mindfulness helps us become more aware, and developing compassion for ourselves and others helps us be more forgiving of unconscious bias. The model below is useful for surfacing bias.

### Try this: 'Halos and Horns' model

#### 30 Minutes

The 'Halos and Horns' model[11] was developed by leadership coach and coach supervisor Eve Turner, as an easy and simple but powerful tool for systemic reflection, not just in coaching, coaching supervision and mentoring but also in management and leadership. The term 'halos and horns' refers to an effect Eve studied when she was a leader working in the BBC. The term suggests that in selection and recruitment interviews, for example, we make quick judgements (possibly due to unconscious bias and counter-transference) about a candidate and then seek out the information that supports our initial view. Our rapid judgements can be linked to appearance, someone's voice, someone they remind us of, and so on, and aren't necessarily valid predictors of performance.

## Objectives

- Surfacing patterns and themes that we might otherwise miss if we just consider individual elements or people
- Allowing deeper exploration of unconscious biases and other unhelpful dynamics
- Identifying when we get 'triggered' by certain people, resulting in us being less resourceful
- Bringing to the spotlight employees we neglect or misjudge, unconsciously applying 'halos and horns'
- Offering more choice in how we respond and react and interact

- **Step 1**
  Use the practice outlined on page 8, 'Getting mindful', to get into an intentioned mindset for the exercise.
- **Step 2**
  Use Table 3 to bring to mind people you coach, lead or manage. Complete each of the columns. The second, 'Halo or horns or unsure', refers to whether when we bring a certain person to mind, we cast them as 'good' or 'bad'.

  Questions to consider:
  - Who are we drawn to?
  - Who are we antagonized by?
  - What are our reflex reactions?
  - What is it that makes certain people easier for us to work with or coach?
  - What can we learn from these reflections that will help us be better leaders, managers and coaches?

## Table 3: The 'Halos and Horns' Model

Source: © Eve Turner Associates, 2019[12]

| 1. Client (initials) | 2. Halo or horns or unsure (would the organization see them the same way?) | 3. Parent, Adult or Child (Transactional Analysis see page 97): how I see them and how I see myself in the relationship | | 4. Parent, Adult or Child: my ratio as coach/team leader in sessions with client/team member (e.g. P 25%, A 70%, C 5%) | | 5. Drama (Karpman, see page 98) Triangle: do the client or I ever step onto the triangle and become Rescuer, Persecutor or Victim (with us/others)? | | 6. Brief description– physical sensations I have, image, metaphor, magical creature, historical character, dance we do etc. | 7. Emerging themes |
|---|---|---|---|---|---|---|---|---|---|
| | | Me | Them | Actual % | Desired % | Me | Them | | |
| | | | | | | | | | |
| | | | | | | | | | |
| | | | | | | | | | |
| | | | | | | | | | |
| | | | | | | | | | |
| | | | | | | | | | |

- **Step 3**
  Capture any additional reflections on patterns that
  emerge. You can then explore these patterns with
  others, but make sure you don't identify anyone!

---

However, awareness of the existence of bias doesn't always
lead to behavioural change.[13] So, what can you or those you
coach do? Feedback can be a useful tool.

- **Get independent feedback**
  This may be from colleagues, or from external coaches
  you allow to 'shadow' you at work and who can help you
  surface biases in coaching sessions. Shadow coaching
  can be very helpful as the coach isn't part of the same
  system (unless they are an internal coach), so they
  might be able to 'hold up the mirror' more easily than
  colleagues. It can be supplemented by independent,
  professionally facilitated, 360 degrees feedback
  interviews.
- **Ensure others in your team are getting feedback too**
  If you're giving them feedback in coaching
  conversations, remember to be appreciative, grateful
  and accepting.

## Building awareness of relationship dynamics in coaching

It is useful to be aware of certain therapeutic phenomena,
dynamics and processes that may arise in a coaching relationship. They include:

- **Idealization**
  This is where someone puts the other person on a pedestal, endowing them with exceptional qualities in comparison to their own. In coaching, this can lead to the person being coached being overly dependent. If this happens, let them know you think they've exaggerated how wonderful you are, and explore their own strengths and good qualities.

- **Projection**
  This is when we project on to others parts of ourselves that we haven't yet embraced. A common example is when the person being coached feels anxious about their performance and this triggers a critical inner voice. Rather than heal this aspect of themselves, they project on to you, experiencing you as a critical authority figure and possibly becoming angry or upset. If this happens, draw on your mindfulness practice. Avoid blame or defensiveness. Don't get drawn into behaving in the way they're unconsciously inviting you to do. Gently and unthreateningly draw their attention to how you've experienced them.

- **Competitiveness**
  People's insecurities may manifest as them competing with you as coach.

- **Parallel process**
  This is a dynamic where, when the other person projects on to you aspects of themselves they find intolerable, you unconsciously take them on and identify with them. An example is when someone you're coaching is stressed about meeting deadlines and you internalize this stress, rushing the coaching conversation, speaking fast and not allowing space for reflection.

Or you might find there's counter-transference –
where you project on to the person you're coaching
aspects of your own emotional landscape.

## Transactional Analysis

One framework with which to explore relationship dynamics,
to inform your coaching and explore with those you coach, is
that of Transactional Analysis (TA).

TA, developed by Eric Berne in the 1950s, identifies three ego
states: Parent, Child, Adult. Eric's hypothesis is that, early on
in their lives, people form a 'script' around their beliefs about
who they are, what the world is like, how they relate to the
world and the world to them, and how others treat them. We
play 'games' which are unconsciously motivated behavioural
interactions with the world, our environment and others. The
more aware we become of our negative games, the more we can
choose not to play them, and to change the script. The ideal
in coaching is for all parties to approach one another Adult to
Adult.

In his Drama Triangle drawing on TA, Stephen Karpman
identified three roles in the context of the psychological games
we play in our relationships: the Rescuer, the Victim and the
Persecutor.[14]

The **Rescuer** cares about the Victim's plight, but doesn't own
their own vulnerability or take self-responsibility, instead seeking to rescue people they see as vulnerable. They take over the
Victim's thinking and solving, discounting the Victim's capacity to assess what's needed, take action, and ask for assistance
if required. The Rescuer often ends up feeling resentful, and
that they are the Victim, although others may see them as the
Persecutor.

The **Victim** realizes they're suffering but they believe they're powerless and don't use clear thinking or problem-solving skills. If they feel let down or persecuted by their Rescuer, they'll then adopt the Persecutor position, although they'll still experience themselves as the Victim.

The **Persecutor** is unaware of their own power so they discount it. The power used is negative and often destructive. As with the other positions, any 'player' in the 'game' may adopt this role whilst holding a different internal perception. If the Persecutor is conscious of what they're doing, they're not actually playing the game, they're using a strategy.

Each of the positions is taken up when we discount or fail to own an issue. The remedies, according to Miriam Orriss, co-founder of the Coaching Supervision Academy, are for:

- the **Rescuer** to take responsibility for him/herself, connect with their power and acknowledge their vulnerability
- the **Victim** to own their vulnerability, take responsibility for themselves, recognize that they have power and use it appropriately, and
- the **Persecutor** to own their power, rather than be afraid of it or use it covertly.

Remember that although we may recognize ourselves particularly in one role, we all switch. For example, the Persecutor may feel guilty about how they've behaved, so they become the Rescuer.

Watch out for those we coach or work with playing the Victim role and trying to 'hook' us into helping them. If we don't engage, they'll look for someone else to play the 'game' or try another game as Persecutor – maybe saying something negative about your coaching or leadership skills!

## The Winner's Triangle

Acey Choy devised an alternative triangle, with more healthy dynamics.[15] In his Winner's Triangle:

- The Victim adopts the **Vulnerable Person Role** who, whilst suffering or having the potential to do so, accesses Adult problem-solving skills, and has the awareness to tune into their feelings as a source of data about necessary changes. They may, as part of their problem solving, seek support.

  Key skill: *problem solving*.

- The Rescuer becomes the **Caring Role** who differs from the former because they respect the other person's ability and they don't take over unless asked, or they want to. They use their capacity for awareness to monitor their own needs and feelings so they can decide if they're willing to assist and in which capacity. If not, they can decline without guilt.

  Key skill: *listening*.

- The Persecutor becomes the **Assertive Role** who still wants their needs met but, unlike the former, has no interest in using their energy to punish, and they don't relish any suffering they may cause.

  Key skill: *negotiating*.

Now let's widen our focus from coaching individuals to coaching the team.

# 8  Coaching Your Team

> 'We cling to the myth of the Lone Ranger, the romantic
> idea that great things are usually accomplished by
> a larger-than-life individual working alone. Despite
> evidence to the contrary – including the fact that
> Michelangelo worked with a group of sixteen to paint
> the Sistine Chapel – we still tend to think of achievement
> in terms of the Great Man or Great Woman, instead of
> the great group.'
> – Warren Bennis, leadership expert, 1997

## When to coach the team

I advise that for complex deep work with the team as a whole,
you engage a professional team coach. Even better, engage a
pair of team coaches – it's easier for two to hold a 'safe space' for
the team and to manage and hold the mirror to the dynamics.

That said, leaders and managers are increasingly and effectively engaging in team coaching.

## Team coaching issues to explore

How might you support the team as a whole, and which issues can you support the team with? Your work as team coach may include helping the team in some or all of the following areas, identified as vital by David Clutterbuck, visiting professor in coaching at the University of Sheffield Hallam and the University of Oxford.[1]

- Discovering the team's identity
- Clarifying what it wants to achieve and why
- Accepting what it can't or shouldn't do, and understanding its potential to achieve
- Understanding its critical processes, including how decisions are made and how team members communicate effectively with one another
- Accessing creativity and innovation
- Boosting collective resilience, including improving collective emotional well-being and management, and moderating responses to success and setbacks
- Monitoring its own progress

In addition, you may be supporting the team to address challenges such as those identified below by Peter Hawkins, leadership coach and prolific author, which he sees as reflecting wider global challenges.[2]

- Managing expectations of all the different stakeholders, particularly given that, as leader or manager, you can feel you're the intersection of these conflicting demands

- Engaging the commitment of these different stakeholders
- Managing challenges arising in the interconnections, the interfaces and relationships between people, teams, functions and different stakeholder needs
- Increasing team capacity for working through systemic conflict
- Learning to live with multiple demands on team members' loyalty in a world that has become more interconnected and in organizations that have become more matrixed
- Finding space to stand back and reflect on the bigger picture, given that the world is becoming more complex and interconnected
- Managing the impacts of the growth of virtual working, such as on the ability to build and sustain trust

Let's explore some ways to increase team effectiveness and resilience.

### Laying the foundations
It's important to start with the foundations. You'll need to apply the core competencies, adapting them for team coaching. Make sure that you meet the ethical, legal and professional guidelines outlined previously.

### Co-creating agreements
Coaching the team requires establishing an agreement that is co-created and agreed with the team, ensuring all team members understand the purpose and hoped-for outcomes of the coaching overall, and any one-off coaching exercises.

### The Conscious Coaching mindset

As well as putting the core attitudes in place ourselves, in terms of how we work with the team, encourage others to do the same. Explain the attitudes to them and encourage them to embody them.

---

## Try this: Exploring core attitudes

### 20 Minutes

- **Step 1**
  Write/draw each of the attitudes on a piece of card.
- **Step 2**
  Divide your team into pairs or groups. Invite them to explore what these attitudes (one or a handful, depending on the number of team members) mean to them individually and as a team. Ask the following questions:
  - *How could they bring these attitudes into the team and into the workplace in general?*
  - *Are there any other attitudes they think are missing but necessary?*
  - *What might be the benefits of bringing in these attitudes?*
- **Step 3**
  Explore in the group/team as a whole.

---

### Co-creating the right relationships

Many of the elements here are the same as when coaching one-to-one.

## Presence

If we've practised developing and maintaining presence with individuals, we can put it to great use with our teams. Again, we need to be flexible, probably more so, and able to dance in the moment. We need to access and trust our intuition and inner wisdom, and be comfortable with not-knowing and experimentation. We need to role-model these attitudes and competencies.

It's helpful if we can use humour as well – it's a great tool for getting people on board and to create energy shifts.

## Rapport

Building and maintaining rapport, and interest, can be more challenging with a group or team than it is one-to-one, because there's more going on. Watch out for:

- feeling a lack of warmth and openness from either the whole team or certain people
- people looking away and fidgeting
- you feeling restless and uncomfortable or detached from the team
- the energy in the room dipping – this can be more noticeable in a whole group or team than one-to-one.

Just as you might when coaching one-to-one, if you notice a lack of rapport, you can call it out. And just as you might do in coaching individuals, if you've been working with the team for some time and things aren't taking off, ask the team what's happening. You should review from time to time anyway. Suggest a review, and ask them:

- What's working well for us?
- What's not working so well?

## Establishing trust and mutual respect

This is equally if not more important when working with the team. We heard earlier how creating psychological safety and trust are key to the success of teams.

Below are the steps taken by Google's head of industry Paul Santagata to boost psychological safety.[3]

- Approach conflict as a collaborator, not an adversary, looking for mutually beneficial outcomes.
- Speak human to human, reminding the team that even in contentious negotiations, the other party also wants to walk away happy.
- Anticipate reactions and plan countermoves.
- Replace blame with curiosity.
- Ask for feedback on delivery.
- Measure psychological safety. Some teams at Google ask questions such as, 'How confident are you that you won't receive retaliation or criticism if you admit an error or make a mistake?'

## Developing compassion and kindness

We saw earlier some of the key benefits of developing compassion. They include creating fertile conditions for flourishing and enabling relationships. Below are some exercises to help you do this for yourself and others.

# Try this: Compassion-focused imagery exercise

## 10 Minutes

This exercise is adapted from one developed by Paul Gilbert for use in Compassion-Focused Therapy.[4]

### Objectives

- To feel our way into directing compassion to ourselves, offering a gentle way of doing so, and to build up our capacity
- **Step 1**
  Use the practice outlined on page 8, 'Getting mindful', to get into an intentioned mindset for the exercise.
- **Step 2**
  Reflecting on what are the ideal qualities or attributes of someone (imagined or real) who's compassionate. Bringing to mind an object, image, person (imagined or real), deity that aligns with your initial ideal of compassionate qualities. Ask yourself:
  - What other core compassionate qualities are represented (for example, caring-commitment, wisdom, strength)?
  - What can you see? Hear? Feel?

  You or those you coach can draw on this image when facing a challenge, reflecting on what they would say to you and how they would act in this situation. You can gradually start to practise embodying the image's compassionate qualities.

# Try this: Self-compassion break

**5 Minutes**

Self-compassion has three core components: mindfulness, common humanity and kindness. Once you've got the hang of compassion-focused imagery, and you feel able and willing to have a go at directing compassion inwards, try this little practice, developed by compassion expert Kristin Neff. I share this with leader clients as a way to bring to life the three components in a useful in-the-moment application.

## Objectives

- Accessing a 'pocket' practice for self-compassion in the moment
- Building your capacity to self-soothe and be self-compassionate
- Building resilience

- **Step 1**
  Bringing your mind to a mildly stressful scenario.
- **Step 2**
  Saying to yourself, 'This is a moment of suffering' (here we call upon **mindfulness**, naming whatever it is, turning towards whatever it is). Playing around with language that works for you personally, for example, 'This is actually quite hard.'
- **Step 3**
  Saying to yourself, 'Suffering is a part of life' (here we call upon **common humanity**, the idea that we all suffer, we're not alone).

- **Step 4**
  Asking yourself, 'May I be kind to myself in this moment?' (this is about **kindness**). Try placing your hands over your heart and imagining what you would say to a friend. Maybe, 'I'm here for you.'
- **Step 5**
  Now letting go of the practice, noticing how you feel, allowing yourself to just be for a while.

## Try this: Loving kindness meditation

### 5 Minutes

In addition to promoting well-being and connection, opening up to our heart gives us access to things we may not otherwise have thought of.

### Objectives

- Enhancing resilience, empathy and self-compassion[5]
- Driving positive behavioural change[6]
- Rewriting internal scripts[7]
- Quietening our inner critic, becoming more present and listening more deeply to the person you're coaching, creating an environment which improves coaching outcomes and supporting more transformational work[8]

There are variations of the loving kindness meditation. Here is one.

- **Step 1**
  Use the practice outlined on page 8, 'Getting mindful', to get into an intentioned mindset for the exercise.
- **Step 2**
  Saying to yourself, 'May I be safe . . . may I be kind to myself . . . may I be free from suffering . . . may I accept myself as I am.'
- **Step 3**
  Bringing to mind someone you love or like, and imagining saying to them, 'May you be safe . . . may you be kind to yourself . . . may you be free from suffering . . . may you accept yourself as you are'.
- **Step 4**
  Choosing someone who doesn't arouse strong feelings either way – someone 'neutral' – and imagining saying to them, 'May you be safe . . . may you be kind to yourself . . . may you be free from suffering . . . may you accept yourself as you are.'
- **Step 5**
  Now someone you find a bit difficult (not too difficult), and again, imagining saying to them, 'May you be safe . . . may you be kind to yourself . . . may you be free from suffering . . . may you accept yourself as you are.' It can help to imagine them as a young child and to consider that, just like everyone, they want to be happy.
- **Step 6**
  Finally, imagining everyone in the place you work, or even the whole nation, or world, and saying to them, 'May you all be safe . . . may you all be kind to yourselves . . . may you all be free from suffering . . . may you all accept yourselves as you are.'

- **Step 7**
  Bringing the practice to an end, noticing what's happening in your Triangle of Awareness, and making any notes you feel will be useful.

## Managing relationship dynamics and avoiding pitfalls

We looked at some examples of relationship dynamics earlier. You'll probably see plenty of these in the team. You might find that some of the following scenarios play out.

- One or more team members **idealize** you, putting you on a pedestal, over-estimating your strengths and good qualities at the expense of their own. Edifying though this may be, resist the urge to wallow in the praise, and flag up what others have to offer.
- One or more team members **project** aspects of themselves on to you.
- People become **competitive**. They may compete with you or other team members. Maybe one of the team members will try to step up as an alternative leader/manager.
- **Parallel process**. One or more team members might manifest frustration or anger with the process or project, and you might find you take this on without realizing it's not coming from you.

In teams, we'll see plenty of 'games' being played (in Trans-actional Analysis terms), with team members shifting from playing different roles.

Becoming aware of potential relationship dynamics and the games people are playing (including you) will help you avoid getting 'hooked' into playing someone else's game, and you'll be more able to spot when others are doing the same. That way, you'll increase your own and the team's effectiveness.

You can work with the 'Halos and Horns' model I shared earlier to help you:

- identify the hidden biases you're holding and judgements you're making about individual team members, so you can address these and become more resourceful
- treat team members more equally and bring to the spotlight those you neglect or misjudge
- surface patterns and themes in the team, identifying when you get 'triggered' by certain people, resulting in you being less resourceful

## Watch out for canaries

Sometimes one person acts like the canary in the pit – signalling something that's wrong in the system. Make sure you don't make them into a scapegoat. Ask the team what's going on for them. Likewise, you might notice an increase in energy and might want to get curious about that – it can signal something you could do more of as a team, some inspiring ideas or next steps.

## Facilitative style

It's just as important, or more so, in team coaching as it is in one-to-one coaching to make use of a facilitative style. Remember, the mantra is: 'Ask, don't tell.'

## Try this: Team coaching moments

### 5 Minutes

From time to time, in team meetings, when you're exploring challenges and possible solutions, introduce coaching moments.

### Objectives

- Encouraging and empowering your team members to think for themselves
- Embedding a coaching style of working together

In pairs, invite them to ask each other, without worrying about being right or wrong:

- Is there anything that's worked well for *you* before that could work here?
- What do *you* think would be a possible solution?

## Communication techniques

You can adapt all of the communication techniques you've learnt for one-to-one coaching for working with your team: deep listening; clarifying, reflecting and reframing; powerful questioning and use of silence.

### Deep listening

Encourage team members to listen actively by:

- suggesting turning mobiles on to silent mode in team meetings
- explaining the different listening levels and inviting them to try listening more deeply and actively
- leading them through mindfulness practices so they can be more present

## Try this: Team deep listening exercise

### 10 Minutes

You will need a notepad for this exercise.

### Objectives

- Perfecting the art of deep listening
- Accessing more information about what's being said and what's not being said
- Boosting connection with others
- Increasing the chance of people feeling heard and understood

- **Step 1**
  Explain the exercise and its objectives. Ask the team to split into pairs (if there's an odd number, three people can group up, and one observes and feeds back what they noticed).

- **Step 2**
  Lead the team through a brief mindfulness exercise.
  Use the practice outlined on page 8, 'Getting mindful',
  to do this.
- **Step 3**
  Team members to decide who's listening (Listener) and
  who's speaking (Speaker).

  **Round 1**
  **3 Minutes**
  The Listener speaks without being interrupted while
  the Speaker sits back in their chair, relaxed, looking
  them in the eyes, seeing if they can hold the intention
  to just be there for them, no agenda of their own, and
  listening. No interrupting. No advising. Just listening
  deeply with all their senses.

  **Round 2**
  **3 Minutes**
  The pair swap and repeat the exercise in their different
  roles.
- **Step 4**
  The pair, then the whole team, debrief. What did they
  notice? Are there any observations that they can note
  down?

## Clarifying and reflecting

Repeating back or paraphrasing what you've heard team members say will help them feel listened to and understood. Make
sure you include everyone.

## Powerful questioning and use of silence

Asking the team the right kind of questions – simple, clear, open and provocative – can be very powerful as a way to:

- move team members on, or the team as a whole, if they're stuck
- inspire the team
- reveal new ways of approaching something and discover innovative solutions and next steps
- consider the bigger picture.

Use silence – including in mindfulness practices – to help team members think without being interrupted, and to recharge.

# Structuring team coaching interventions and designing actions

Here you'll learn:

- how to work effectively with goal setting in the team
- how to structure team coaching interventions.

## Goal setting

You can use any of the models shared earlier for goal setting and planning for a whole team coaching session or meeting, or as part of a meeting. Here's a reminder of what we explored earlier.

- **GROW** (**G**oal, **R**eality, **O**ptions, **W**ill/Wrap-up): make sure you don't spend too much time exploring the current reality, especially if you're hearing from all the team members.

- **EXACT** (Explicit (succinct and one focus); eXciting (positively framed and inspiring); Assessable (measurable); Challenging (stretching); and Time-framed (preferably within three to six months): make sure everyone is in agreement around what will inspire and stretch *all* team members.
- **The 'four-eyed' model** (Intention, Ideas, Inspiration, Initiation): give everyone a chance to share ideas and identify which ones they find inspiring.

Here are some tips for effective team goal setting.

- Co-create and agree goals and outcomes with the team so they have ownership
- Build in accountability to each other for making things happen
- Remember not to hold on too tightly to goals, particularly in these ambiguous and unpredictable times
- Sit with not-knowing and let things emerge
- Let multiple perspectives surface and multiple voices be heard
- Show appreciation and gratitude
- Celebrate any achievements

## Structuring team coaching sessions and meetings

Below is a framework for structuring a team coaching session or meeting, inspired by Peter Hawkins' CID-CLEAR model.[9]

Hawkins originally created the CLEAR model as a framework for coaching interventions, outlining five stages of progression.

1 Contracting
2 Listening
3 Exploring
4 Action
5 Review

He then added another three stages to his framework specifically for team coaching. These stages (CID) represent the initial explorations involved in team coaching.

1 Contracting
2 Inquiries
3 Diagnosis

### Working with the CID-CLEAR model

As with other coaching models, such as GROW or FELT, the flow isn't always linear. Use your intuition and judgement to decide whether it's worth spending more time in one stage than usual.

## Try this: CID-CLEAR

- **Step 1**
  Getting mindful: lead the team through a brief mindfulness exercise. Use the practice outlined on page 8, 'Getting mindful', to do this.
- **Step 2**
  Contracting: exploring why coaching is needed. There are a number of potential parties who might be

involved in such an exploration – team leader and team members, team coach (could be an external coach or the leader or manager-as-coach) and their boss.

- **Step 3**
Inquiry: What's going on in the team? This might typically include exploring what kind of team the team is and may consist of holding semi-structured meetings with team members, sending out a team 360-degree feedback instrument to all key stakeholders and talking to the most critical stakeholders, collecting data on performance and functioning, and team members completing questionnaires such as Belbin team role analysis.[10]

- **Step 4**
Diagnosis (and design): this involves analysing all the data to allow the focus for team coaching to become clear, and to start mapping out a possible coaching journey.

Having completed the initial explorations, you move on to CLEAR (you can use the CLEAR framework below for one-to-one coaching too).

- **Step 5**
Getting mindful: lead the team through a brief mindfulness exercise. Use the practice outlined on page 8, 'Getting mindful', to do this.

- **Step 6**
Checking in and Contracting. Ask your team: How are we today? What do we need to achieve today? What would success look like, and how can we work together to achieve it? Now's the time to share any salient points from the inquiry and initial diagnosis. Then co-design

and agree objectives, process and the programme for
the coaching.

- **Step 7**
Listening: listen to updates and new challenges,
different perspectives, hopes and fears (you can
introduce a brief mindfulness practice so people
can notice more than they otherwise would, or the
multiple perspectives model to access a richer range of
perspectives).

 Tune in not only to what's being discussed and
reported, but to what's going on in patterns of
behaviour, emotions being expressed (including
through non-verbal communication) and assumptions,
mindsets and motivations that seem to be underneath
the words and how they're said.

 *Mindful twist:* Draw on mindfulness techniques
to deepen your listening – be explicit with the rest
of the team about this, invite them to join you for a
brief mindfulness practice at the beginning of the
meeting. When you're listening in, notice what's going
on internally for you, for additional data. Then play
back what's come up for you – mindfully and with
kindness.

- **Step 8**
Exploring and Experimenting: brainstorm all the
elements that might be needed to progress (or focus on
one or two specific issues). What can we experiment
with today?

 In team coaching, what you do here will obviously
depend on what's come up from the inquiry, and the
objectives.

- **Step 9**

  **A**ction: lots of energy and insights have hopefully been generated. The trick is to translate these into next steps. Which actions and new behaviours can we commit to? By when, and with the support of whom? What can we do right now?

  *Mindful twist*

  Incorporate the L part of the FELT model introduced earlier: What do we want to keep and **let be**? What do we want to **let go of**? What new ways of thinking/ being/behaving/doing do we want to **let in**? What will success be like? You might want to lead the team through the Exploring part of the FELT model too for this last stage. Ask them to tap into what will be different, and to notice what they're feeling, thinking, observing bodily sensations, what their senses tell them. What can they see, hear? Exploring in this way helps embed any shifts.

- **Step 10**

  **R**eview: how are we going to track progress or lack of it? What's working well? What could we do even better? What are people's takeaways? How are you faring in terms of attaining desired team improvements?

  Bring in some appreciation, inviting team members to share what others have contributed and brought to the table. And do the same yourself, of course.

## Accessing new perspectives

You can use all the exercises I shared in the chapters on one-to-one coaching to help your team come up with new perspectives and ideas, boosting creativity and innovation. Below are some adaptations for teams, and some new exercises to inspire you and others.

**Letting go**

Letting go (page 47) can be a good place to start. As teams, we can get very attached to how we've always done things. It can be hard to let go of old ways and bring in the new.

Try inviting all the team to go through the steps outlined previously, practising letting go of what's gone before.

---

## Try this: Mindful multiple perspectives for your team

### 30–40 Minutes

You will need a large room for this exercise.

### Objectives

- Helping to let go of old ways and beliefs
- Opening up to new solutions

- **Step 1**
  Together identify a topic that you'd like to investigate
- **Step 2**
  Identify one person to guide the process (Facilitator).
- **Step 3**
  Getting mindful: lead the team through a brief mindfulness exercise. Use the practice outlined on page 8, 'Getting mindful', to do this.

- **Step 4**
  The Facilitator leads the others through each perspective stage in turn, inviting people to move around the room to a different spot for each stage.
- **Step 5**
  After going through all the perspectives, invite people to sit back down and allow a couple of minutes for them to take notes on what they noticed and any insights.
- **Step 6**
  Take turns to share what came up from each perspective (some perspectives may not have prompted anything, which is fine). As each person talks, the others just listen deeply.
- **Step 7**
  Identify any next steps.

## Try this: Mindful systemic constellations for your team

Systemic constellation exercises can work well with teams, and groups too, but only if those present don't know anything about what's being enquired into. And there needs to be lots of space in the room.

- **Step 1**
  Identify one person to guide the process (Enquirer).

- **Step 2**
  Getting mindful: lead the team through a brief
  mindfulness exercise. Use the practice outlined on
  page 8, 'Getting mindful', to do this.
- **Step 3**
  The Enquirer chooses people to represent specific
  elements related to the enquiry – people who don't
  know anything about the question or the elements.
  It's important to be sensitive around confidentiality if
  exploring relationship dynamics.
- **Step 4**
  The Enquirer moves the people to positions and places
  that best represent his/her inner image of the situation.
- **Step 5**
  The representatives speak up about what they're
  sensing and observing. They may feel drawn to moving
  somewhere else, in which case they should do so.
- **Step 6**
  What patterns have emerged? What needs to shift?
  What steps need to be taken?

## Try this: Gregersen brainstorming process

### 10–12 Minutes

You will need a timer for this exercise.

Hal Gregersen, innovative leadership expert, and
executive director of the MIT Leadership Center and
senior lecturer at the MIT Sloan School of Management,

is a keen advocate of catalytic questions. His three-step Question Burst approach proposes brainstorming questions (not answers) around a specific challenge or opportunity for four minutes with the aim of a team generating 15 to 20 questions. Below we add mindfulness too.

### Objectives

- Examining alternative vantage points to arrive at new solutions
- Accessing inner intuition and wisdom

- **Step 1**
  Getting mindful: lead the team through a brief mindfulness exercise. Use the practice outlined on page 8, 'Getting mindful', to do this.
- **Step 2**
  Focus your group's attention on their Triangles of Awareness for two minutes.
- **Step 3**
  Set the stage by selecting a challenge you care deeply about. Invite a few people to help you consider that challenge from fresh angles. Ideally, choose people who have no direct experience with the problem and whose worldview is starkly different from yours. In two minutes or less, share your problem with your partners.
- **Step 4**
  Brainstorm the questions. Set a timer and spend the next four minutes collectively generating as many questions as possible about the challenge. Follow two key rules: 1) don't answer any of the questions, and 2) don't explain why you're asking the questions.

Go for at least 15 to 20 questions in four minutes. Write all the questions down word for word as you hear them.

- **Step 5**
Study the questions and select a few catalytic ones from the list. Commit to pursuing at least one new pathway you've glimpsed.

    *Access additional data and wisdom:* as part of the exploration in this step, also draw on data from your bodies and feelings.

    What do your bodies and hearts tell you?

## The Future Self or Future Team exercise for your team

Leading your team through the Future Self exercise can be fun, as well as empowering them to access their potential and wisdom. You could also invite them to explore how they see the Future Team, using the same process but in addition inviting them to explore what their ideal Future Team would be like.

## Working with stories for your team

In team coaching, draw on the power of storytelling by encouraging team members to identify:

- which stories they as team members, and the team as a whole, are telling themselves, and
- which stories would be more effective and inspiring to embody as a team.

## Art-based coaching for your team

Choose a topic for team members to illustrate, such as the team or organization's vision, team members' or the team's role in relation to others, the team or organization's purpose, and so on.

If you're doing this with the team, remind them it's not about drawing beautifully. Get team members to pair up and discuss what they've drawn.

## Shifting location
Shake things up by taking your team to a new location – maybe even the streets – and lead them through the location coaching, urban coaching and cultural coaching processes outlined earlier. You might set them the task of exploring a particular issue. It can be fun and energizing for your team members, and can help them access different perspectives.

## The FELT model for your team
The FELT model can be used in team/group coaching and gatherings to mindfully explore the following.

- A specific issue
- Emotions that you sense are being held back in the team
- Wisdom being signalled by team members' bodies
- A new mindset, way of being, vision or strategy

Go through the same steps outlined earlier for FELT but if you're working with a team or group, lead them through the process in silence. It can be used with a large group to explore how they feel about a change initiative and/or to surface insight about a new strategy, or flesh out a vision for the future, and so on, in which case you set the topic for the enquiry.

## *Building team resilience*
Another way to smooth and build relationships is to foster team mindfulness, although it brings other benefits too, including creating psychological safety.

In the workplace, collective mindfulness is much more than the sum of individual mindfulness. According to research by Cranfield University and the Institute of Employment Studies, collective mindfulness-based interventions additionally:

- build organizational readiness for change
- support innovative or disruptive ways of working, and
- improve resilience and adaptability to the world's growing complexity.[11]

Further research by the IES and Cranfield published in 2019 explored the benefits of mindfulness within the team environment, drawing on research within the UK defence sector,[12] commissioned to explore if mindfulness could be leveraged for strategic benefits. As an IES associate, I was part of the research team. It was a fascinating project.

## CASE STUDY

### The British Military

The UK defence sector has recognized that the world of work, workers and warfare will have undergone a transformative change by 2040. The rate of change is likely to increase before then, and individuals and teams working in defence will need to be resilient, agile, have a learning orientation and be 'change-ready' on a continuous basis.

Prompted by this realization, as part of the Defence Science and Technology Laboratory's 'Strategic Edge Through People 2040' project, a research team from the IES and Cranfield was commissioned to investigate if, and how, mindfulness could be leveraged for strategic benefits.

The team examined and compared different types of mindfulness-based mental fitness training – an individual mindfulness meditation training programme and a newly designed team mindfulness training programme – to determine effectiveness in generating improved resilience, cognitive capacity and team work.

The team training programme encouraged participant behaviours, including:

- paying attention to what's changing around them day to day
- continuously watching out for each other so that others can step in if someone starts to struggle (to increase organizational resilience), and
- questioning collective assumptions.

Both programmes promoted individual well-being and resilience.

A flight lieutenant from the Royal Air Force said, 'Mindfulness enables us to address retention of personnel plus better mental health and well-being plus better resilience plus moral discipline. All in one go. Plus enable more diverse teams to operate effectively.'

However, the team programme, in addition to being significantly more popular, delivered wider strategic benefits, such as:

- improved team communication
- improved team-working skills, and
- dealing with conflict constructively.

Participants identified occasions during challenging team situations when a team member would suggest applying individual or team-focused mindfulness techniques learnt in training. The rest of the team would follow their instruction, resulting in more effective team functioning.

An officer cadet from the British Royal Naval College in Dartmouth said, 'One member of the group identified that we were becoming argumentative and brash with each other, so we decided to collectively do some breathing exercises together. This resulted in us all being a lot calmer, so we could be more productive and begin to work out what to do.'

Key messages from the research included that individual mindfulness meditation is only one way to enhance mindfulness. Due to its self-help connotations, meditation alone may be perceived as less universally appealing in the military, where dedication, service and self-sacrifice are important values. It recommends that the military should consider mindfulness as a team activity, fostering team cultures in which everyone is encouraged to consistently notice the needs and reactions of others, especially in the face of stress, and to create collaborative, collective solutions to challenges and complex threats.

---

## Cultivating a mindful and compassionate team
The objectives are to increase:

- connection and rapport
- resilience and change-readiness
- agility and adaptability in unpredictable times
- focus and clarity
- emotional intelligence.

Here are some strategies that will help you to develop a mindful, compassionate team, with the benefits outlined above.

- Make mindfulness and compassion part of the language of the team. Bring in a trained mindfulness teacher to teach the team how to be mindful and compassionate (see Appendix 1 for tips on finding teachers) as individual members and as a team.
- Treat stress as a collective challenge. Encourage team members to systematically anticipate and adapt collectively when conflict around tasks risks escalating into relationship conflict, and put in place protocols, routines or regular processes to notice and talk about how their behaviour and needs might change when they're under pressure. Encourage team members to check in more frequently with each other and notice when a member is struggling. (What do you/we need? How can we support each other? How can we be more mindful and compassionate?) Create a routine or regular process that enables people.
- Help the team practise resolving small and successively more important conflicts constructively.
- Create a team culture built on interpersonal trust and mutual respect, independent of rank, background or experience, where anyone can at an appropriate time speak truth to power.
- Introduce the team to the core Conscious Coaching attitudes.
  *Tip:* write each attitude on a piece of card and get different pairs or groups to discuss one or a few of the attitudes, then discuss in the team. (How can you bring these into the work you do? What might be the benefits?)
- Start team meetings and punctuate long meetings with brief mindfulness practices – awareness of breath,

SOAR (page 162), or mindful walking (suggesting team members take a short mindful walking break so they come back refreshed).

- Take the meeting outside, or suggest a break outside in nature to boost creative problem solving and clarity, and improve mood.
- Introduce your team to the Triangle of Awareness as a regular practice to help members feel heard, and access more data. As part of team coaching sessions, or in team meetings, ask the team what's going on for them in terms not only of thoughts, but also emotions and bodily sensations.
- Focus specifically on compassion development, leading team members through the compassion-focused imagery exercise (page 107) and the self-compassion break (page 108) shared earlier.
- Lead your team through the appreciation reflection (page 52). (What do team members appreciate about one another? What do you appreciate about them?)
- If there's already rapport, try leading the team through FELT.
- Invite them to explore how they can manage and boost their energy, such as through the nourishing and depleting exercise (see below for team adaptation).

## Try this: Nourishing and depleting exercise for your team

In the section later on which outlines how to coach people around mental health issues, I share the nourishing and depleting exercise (see page 161). You can adapt that

exercise for team members to help them become more
resilient by identifying what drains them and what gives
them energy in their lives, and in team activities and
tasks. Invite team members to answer the following
questions.

- What depletes them?
- What gives them energy?
- Can any helpful changes be made, such as in task
  allocation, time management, getting additional
  training or CPD, delegating?
- How do they support each other and keep each other
  accountable?

# 9  Establishing a Conscious Coaching Culture

> 'Why do we always come back to swim in the same old pond, even though it's mucky, just because it's "ours"?'
> – Vietnamese expression[1]

It's so easy to carry on doing things a certain way just because that's how they've always been done. Changing culture requires intention, commitment, time and patience. Now let's look at rippling Conscious Coaching beyond the team, into the very fabric and culture of the organization.

Here's what we'll explore in this chapter.

- What do we mean by a Conscious Coaching culture? What are the signs of such a culture?
- How to build coaching, mindfulness and compassion into the organization's DNA.

## What do we mean by a coaching culture?

David Megginson and David Clutterbuck, co-founders of the professional body the European Mentoring and Coaching Council, describe it as one in which: 'coaching is a predominant style of managing and working together and where a commitment to grow the organisation is embedded in a parallel commitment to grow the people in the organisation.'[2]

In other words, it's a culture in which a majority of employees use a coaching approach, with each other and external stakeholders and customers, where coaching is 'part of the way we do things around here'. It's not a means in itself.

Despite all the hype, not that many organizations actually have a strong coaching culture, although many aspire to having one, and many have taken lots of steps in the right direction.

It's often said that leaders get the culture they behave rather than the culture they want to see. So, of course, leaders role-modelling a coaching way of being is key and is a clear sign of an organization at least being on the way to having a coaching culture. What are the other signs?

## What do we mean by a Conscious Coaching culture?

It's one which actively develops and embeds coaching, mindfulness and compassion.

### Signs of a strong Conscious Coaching culture
- Senior leaders champion coaching
- Coaching is seen as a key leadership and management competency
- Employees value coaching
- Use of external coach practitioners
- Internal coaches and managers/leaders are trained in coaching skills

- Managers, leaders and internal coaches receive accredited coach training and continuous professional coach development
- Coaching is a fixture with a dedicated line item in the budget
- All employees have equal access to coaching from a professional coach
- Managers look for opportunities to help others to learn rather than just to tackle poor performance
- People ask each other open questions
- All employees have open, honest and supportive conversations
- Teams have clear goals, roles, processes and relationships
- Compassion is shown and embodied in ways including:
  - being alive to the suffering of others
  - rather than merely tolerating those in personal distress, supporting them systemically and through small acts of kindness
  - encouraging and taking appropriate action in the face of suffering
  - encouraging non-judgement, tolerance and appreciation[3]
- Collective organizational mindfulness becomes 'a shared social practice in an organization'[4] including, as prominent collective mindfulness researcher and US organizational theorist Karl Edward Weick describes, through an 'ability of the workforce to be sensitive to changes in the work environment, continuously updating the way in which they think and perceive things', and 'by appreciating the importance of context'.[5] At group level, employees are expected to be capable of

noticing new or developing variables within the system, to be 'collectively mindful'.

## Steps to embedding a Conscious Coaching culture
- **Step 1:** Exploring if now is the right time
- **Step 2:** Co-creating the purpose and values
- **Step 3:** Developing the strategy
- **Step 4:** Getting senior leaders on board
- **Step 5:** Rolling the approach out
- **Step 6:** Ensuring sustainability

Let's explore these six steps in turn.

## Is it the right time for your organization?
- How ready and receptive are people to doing things differently? New practices need time for learning to become embedded, so introduce them when people will be most receptive and have capacity.
- Is the business as a whole ready for a Conscious Coaching approach?
- What are your reasons for introducing it?

## Co-creating the purpose and values
Create a clear and inspiring vision for the culture, considering the following.

- What's the context?
- How will the culture help deliver strategy?
- What's in it for leaders, managers and other employees, for customers/shareholders, the environment, and future generations?

- How can you co-create the vision and values with all employees so there's ownership?
- What's in place already in terms of coaching, mindfulness and compassion?

## Developing the strategy

- Build a strategy aligned with the overarching business strategy and organizational culture.
- Communicate this clearly and frequently.

## Getting senior leaders on board

Developing and sustaining a Conscious Coaching culture will only be achieved through support and a clear vision from senior leaders. In keeping with the facilitative empowering style of coaching, senior leaders will need to consistently give up a fair amount of power to leaders and employees at lower levels.

If you're a senior leader, make sure you're championing Conscious Coaching, and share your story.

## CASE STUDY

## Euroclear's story

Senior buy-in has been vital in growing a small coaching and mentoring pilot in financial organization Euroclear into a successful company-wide initiative across eleven countries.

The initiative saw Euroclear's head of coaching and mentoring, Tim Dench, win *Coaching at Work* magazine's Internal Coaching/ Mentoring Champion 2018 Award. He shared how the then CEO had decided the business needed to be more proactive around culture change, getting Tim on board, which led him to focus on coaching. The business now has its own coach training centre, accredited by the Institute of Leadership & Management to deliver ILM Level 5 coaching, and its team coaching course is ILM-endorsed. 'We wouldn't have got this far if we hadn't had such a strong support from the senior leaders,' says Tim.

---

## Rolling the approach out

- **Be prepared to call in external experts.**
  There's often more reliance on external coaches and external support in the early days of creating a coaching culture, but it reduces as you train up internal coaches and/or mentors, as well as leaders who use a coaching approach in their daily lives. With mindfulness and compassion, at first it's best to bring in trained mindfulness teachers to roll out training, but you can then train up people internally.

- **Combine external and internal expertise.**
  One hallmark of a strong coaching culture is having a strong bench of both internal and external coaches. As external coaches aren't part of the organizational system, they can bring in new and important insights and surface blind spots. And senior leaders may prefer to work with someone from outside. External coaches should be accredited, supervised and experienced, and a good fit for the culture. And they should be sufficiently challenging to be able to support senior leaders.

  It's a good idea to bring the community of external coaches together regularly – with internal coaches, if possible – to update them on what's going on across the organization and to harness learning from common themes emerging. With the latter, it's vital to protect confidentiality.

- **Choose training programmes carefully.**
  When it comes to training, as there are specific skills relating to coaching, mindfulness and compassion, you have a number of options.
  - Offer training separately, providing coach skills training and mindfulness (with compassion woven in), or mindfulness and compassion development as two different options.
  - Weave training programmes together, for example as Conscious Coaching combining core coaching skills, and a module either on mindfulness and compassion, or modules on each.

  Specific compassion skills training programmes include Stanford University's Compassion Cultivation Training, or Compassion Focused Therapy programmes.
- **Don't be elitist.**
  Ensure interventions are not limited to senior executives.
- **Identify current challenges and pitch accordingly, tailor making, pitching and packaging training appropriately.**
  Beware of mandating, and know your people. Help them understand how interventions relate to and will benefit them. Getting the pitch right is vital.

  When Google offered mindfulness for stress management, it didn't get take-up. But when it was rebranded as an emotional intelligence offer, its Search Inside Yourself programme became hugely popular. Elsewhere, it could be the opposite, or something else may draw people in, such as sharpening intellectual ability.
- **Give people a chance to 'try before they buy in'.**
  Running taster sessions, 'question and answer' sessions, offering the chance to spell out potential benefits.

- **Roll out interventions beyond individuals.**
  Culture is found in collective relationships – individual development will not, by itself, bring about cultural shift. Ensure that interventions are for teams and departments too.

     A growing number of employers give all managers and leaders basic training in coaching skills, and weave mindfulness into leadership and management development programmes.

---

**CASE STUDY**

## Automotive Fuel Cell Cooperation (AFCC)

AFCC ensured its coaching strategy is truly embedded into its culture by allowing all employees, co-op students and contractors eligible to participate in coaching, and assigning coaches to all new hires as part of their on-boarding process. AFCC won the International Coach Federation's 2017 ICF Prism Award, which honours organizations whose coaching programmes 'yield discernible and measurable positive impacts, fulfil rigorous professional standards, address key strategic goals, and shape organizational culture'.

---

**Ensuring sustainability**

- **Engage in values-based recruitment.**
  Ensure candidates' and new recruits' values are aligned with the organization's.
- **Make expectations clear from the outset.**
  Reinforce the importance of coaching, mindfulness, empathy and compassion in induction programmes.

- **Role-model new behaviours.**
  Workplace behaviours are highly 'infectious' – the best and worst leadership traits spread contagiously through a business, with professionals' behaviours most heavily influenced by those they work with most frequently, often regardless of age (49 per cent) or seniority (46 per cent), according to research from the Institute of Leadership & Management.[6] Some 74 per cent of UK professionals mirror the leadership styles of their colleagues.

  In terms of Conscious Coaching, positive behaviours will include:
  – 'asking, not telling'
  – admitting as leaders and managers that you can't possibly know everything and neither can anyone else in the team
  – truly listening to employees, valuing their wants, needs and contributions, and responding to these
  – getting to know staff as individuals and understanding their skills and strengths
  – encouraging mindful and compassionate behaviours, such as demonstrating care and concern for others
  – showing that expressing emotion, respect and affection are all positive leadership behaviours
  – at times taking courageous decisions about which work can and can't be delivered.
- **Create a conducive work environment.**
  This includes designing work spaces and work processes that minimize unnecessary distractions and interruptions and help promote a sense of mindful attention, flow and productivity, ensuring there are spaces where people can have coaching conversations,

and can take time out. Support regular individual or group practice by offering a range of support options for practising mindfulness, such as:
– a quiet place to practise
– regular drop-in sessions
– weekly encouraging emails
– creating a bespoke intranet page/portal providing access to a range of mindfulness resources such as free or discounted downloadable mindfulness apps.

• **Encourage individuals to embed habits.**
Make use of visual hints and cues reminding people to take mindful pauses, for example.

• **Integrate Conscious Coaching within core organizational processes.**
Take steps such as:
– embedding Conscious Coaching (coaching, becoming mindful, acting compassionately) into training, leadership development and performance appraisals
– building it into strategic planning, decision-making and goal-setting processes
– creating mindfulness touch points along the employee life cycle by anchoring mindfulness practices in recruitment, on-boarding of new employees, leadership and line manager training, coaching and mentoring, performance appraisals, back-to-work interviews, promotions, low performer processes, line manager standards and exit interviews. This will normally involve building an in-house trainer pool and public championing of mindfulness by senior people.

• **Build the evidence-base.**
To ensure ongoing support of the leadership team.

- **Build a community of coaching, mindfulness and compassion advocates.**
- **Embed mindfulness treatment and prevention pathways.**
  Make sure occupational health providers and others are aware of the benefits of mindfulness training, and refer staff to courses.
- **Train employees to deliver coach and mindfulness training.**
- **Reward and recognize compassionate behaviours.**
  Even if they're small gestures, share inspiring stories, and acknowledge compassionate actions. Derby Teaching Hospitals NHS Foundation Trust in the UK has compassion as a core value, and its staff recognition award scheme is focused on recognizing staff who deliver against these values.[7]
- **Challenge behaviours which contradict a compassionate approach.**
  Such behaviours include disrespect, bullying, injustice, self-interest, micro-management, blame culture and incivility.
- **Regularly review.**
  Check in with both external and internal providers, and assess where the organization is on its coaching culture journey. Is the new strategy bringing about the required cultural shift and is it helping the organization achieve its goals? Involve senior executives, HR leaders, representatives from internal and external coaching teams, mindfulness champions, and so on.

## Pinsent Masons

Pinsent Masons has a well-earned reputation for being ahead of the game. 'We're known for being innovative. Our approach at board level is to look over the wall at what's needed in the future, including what clients will be wanting in five to ten years' time,' says Sophie Turner, partner development coach.

The 1,200-strong international law firm was an early champion of environmentally friendly initiatives and schemes to promote greater diversity. It's one of the trailblazers in its approach to mental illness at work – senior leaders share their own struggles, and it has a mental health champion, for example. And it's won and been shortlisted for many awards, including winning Law Firm of the Year in both the 2019 and the 2018 Lawyer Awards and being ranked among the ten most innovative firms in the Asia Pacific region in the FT 2018 Innovative Lawyer Asia Pacific Awards.

So it comes as no surprise that it was an early adopter of coaching, and that it's combining coaching with mindfulness to positive effect, an approach Turner sometimes calls 'slow coaching'.

Pinsent Masons first introduced coaching in 2006, offering partners (leaders) coaching sessions with external coaches. They're still offering these – it has 12 to 15 external coaches on its preferred supplier list at any one time. However, coaching has now become part of the culture, interwoven with a mindfulness approach.

Most of the board members have been introduced to mindfulness, and some have done coaching. Mindfulness is interwoven with leadership development activities, for example, at new partner events, Turner talks about resilience and invites partners to try a mindfulness exercise.

A combination of coaching and mindfulness is underpinning the organization's transformation to a purpose-led business. Around 90 per cent of its 300 or so partners voted in favour of this cultural change initiative in 2018, after the organization identified in 2017 the increasing importance of purpose to defining business success.

'First of all, [having a coaching culture] allowed this shift to come into play and second, coaching plays a key part in how we will implement it over the next year or so,' says Turner. 'Leaders' ability to understand what a purpose-led organization means, and thus the organization's ability to put the project in place, has been helped substantially by our coaching culture. The whole language around openness and enabling others, which for me is coaching language, would have otherwise felt quite alien to many partners.'

The approach is improving decision making and relationships.

'We've seen, in the relationships between partners, greater acceptance in general, more diversity and acceptance of difference, and greater collaboration. We've reduced the fallout from when disagreement happens. Those trigger points where partners throw off emails to each other and get into a verbal spat or close down, which is a more familiar way, have been minimized.

'There's also more trust in the leadership, which I believe is fundamental in any organization, and particularly at a turbulent time when everyone's worried about the economy.'

Coaching by the external coaches and Turner, who also coaches professionally within the business, is person-centred (assuming each person has the capacity and desire to fulfil their potential) and draws on mindful approaches such as Nancy

Kline's Time to Think[8] or Gestalt.[9] Within sessions, partners are often encouraged to use mindfulness-based exercises such as mindful thinking and breathing 'to restore their balance and resilience levels', says Turner.

Generally, mindfulness is not explicitly mentioned. For example, in meetings to support the senior team working on becoming a purpose-led organization, she allows plenty of mindful listening time.

'Although it's not strictly mindfulness, for me it's a mindful approach and this is the next generation of mindfulness. Rather than having a little badge [saying mindfulness], for me it's bigger than that, it's an ethos. It's about being non-reactive, taking time out, and it appeals to the lawyers. We don't get much traction with anything to do with their health. If you say to a lawyer, get more sleep, drink less alcohol, they say, yeah, yeah, yeah! But appeal to their thinking, to their intellect, about how to use their brain at its best, [that's a different story].'

Partners are happy to start meetings in a mindful way. Turner might ask, for example, 'How are people feeling?' or 'What's on your minds right now?' Or in the middle of a coaching conversation with a partner, she might say, 'If we could just stop a moment . . .' and ask them, 'What's resonating for you in the moment?'

'Things I would never have asked even twelve months or so ago, and they're okay with that, because coaching has had time to embed. In the past they would have thought you were batty! When we first started doing the coaching, partners were shy about working with mindfulness, but now they say, "Great!" That in itself is a huge mind shift,' she says.

'It's accumulative. Partners have seen the benefits of mindfulness individually, in the privacy of coaching, and that's expanded out and become part of the language.

'The rationale for the business is enabling partners to be in their best space possible, with that combination of being mindful and thinking mindfully, which is what coaching [drawing on mindfulness] is providing.

'For me, a mindful and a coaching organizational culture are completely intertwined,' she says.

---

## Beyond the organization

> 'If you want to go quickly, go alone. If you want
> to go far, go together.'
> – African proverb

One of the obstacles in getting a coaching culture off the ground is a lack of opportunity for those newly trained in coaching skills to practise. A great way round this is for organizations to create practice networks. These networks also allow employees to access coaching and coaching supervision from people outside the business, offering new insights and getting round the potential problem of people being coached by their line manager, which isn't always ideal. One example is the West Midlands Employers Coaching and Mentoring Pool.[10]

Bringing together leaders and managers from different organizations can also create momentum, leading to systemic change across a whole sector. Such momentum is currently building within the Welsh Government through a combination of coaching, mindfulness training and education on areas such as behavioural insights.

## The Welsh Government

Aberystwyth University in Wales has worked with the Welsh Government to develop a successful 'second wave' mindfulness initiative to boost mindfulness, improve decision making, and support behavioural and systemic change in the public sector.

Between 2013 and early 2019, more than 200 employees from the Welsh Government, including middle managers and 50 or so senior civil servants, mostly directors, from divisions including the Treasury, NHS and Sustainable Futures, took part in the group 'Mindfulness Based Behavioural Insights & Decision Making' programme co-created by Rachel Lilley, a behaviour change and mindfulness academic based at Aberystwyth University.

Delivering and designing the programme, which has been through a number of iterations, is informing Lilley's PhD into how to bring behavioural insights and mindfulness together to support effective policy and change making in the context of the shifting nature of work in the public sector.

'Governments were designed to count things and tell people what to do but they now need to deal with highly complex issues, with multiple and competing stakeholders, and limited resources,' says Lilley.[11]

'In addition, leaders and managers are required to become more relational. Their jobs now involve collaborating, facilitating, understanding, negotiating, and working with perception, emotion and cognition. They're facilitating their own and other people's understanding, bringing together information that's quite complex and from different places, and developing ideas and conclusions from that. They need to see what's in front of them clearly, challenge themselves regularly, intervene, adapt and modify, all in a complex adaptive system,' she says.

'The job has become entirely different in terms of how they operate and the capacities they need to deal with that. Nowadays, there's incredible diversity so even more than ever, they need to have considered what other people are actually seeing as information. They need training in cognition, how people perceive, what an emotion is and how it relates to cognition. I'd argue they need more metacognition and perspective taking, which are quite advanced skills!

'In a nutshell, the issue mindfulness seeks to address [in these programmes] is that in the public policy sector, they're dealing with huge complexity, and they're dealing with the human psyche and they don't know what it is.'

Each programme cohort has received eight sessions over three months, starting with an all-day module. Mindfulness is incorporated as a method of inquiry into participants' thoughts, feelings/emotions and behaviour. The aim is to increase capacity to feel internal physical states and thus become more aware of the emotional states they embody. In addition to standard mindfulness short practices, participants use the Kalapa Leadership Academy mindfulness app. Coaching is also on offer to participants.

Mindfulness practice is combined with learning theories relating to emotion and cognition (including how they're not separable), decision-making and behavioural economics (which incorporates the study of psychology into the analysis of the decision making behind an economic outcome), cognitive bias work,[12] the extended predictive mind, and constructed emotion.[13]

Gaining a deep understanding, for example, of how heuristics (mental shortcuts) and cognitive biases affect work-based decision making, team working, organizational behaviours, stakeholder engagement, diversity and inclusion, and project design and delivery has profound implications for leadership in VUCA times, explains Lilley. It promotes agility and openness, and takes participants to a very deep level of mental capacity. And understanding how emotional states impact engagement, decision making and bias has particular relevance to those designing interventions to facilitate behavioural shifts in others, she says.

Evaluation including pre- and post-programme surveys and interviews, and analysis of participants' narratives with the tool Sensemaker revealed significant increases in participants' awareness of key behavioural insights such as the effect of the surrounding environments, emotions and values and belief systems on shaping behaviour, and significant increases in their mean scores in the mindfulness trait as measured by the Five Facets of Mindfulness Questionnaire.[14]

In one of the exercises on the programme, participants are asked to take turns in listening, noticing what's coming up for them in their own minds (metacognition) whilst attempting to listen.

'[Participants] had a light-bulb moment when they realized they had their own filters and had been filtering the information being given to them and that they'd been sitting in meetings making assumptions that other people were seeing the information in the same way. So for pragmatic purposes, they started to listen.'

# PART THREE

## Taking It Forward

# 10 Potential Obstacles to Effective Coaching

There are a number of things that can get in the way of excellent coaching. Some you can control as coach, others not always – such as the organizational culture. Potential obstacles are likely to be found in three areas.

- **On the side of the coach**
  - Not putting in place core coaching skills – leading rather than facilitating, asking closed questions, not giving the coachee a chance to think, and so on (see Chapter 6).
  - Not being willing or able to work with strong emotions – we will look at how to do this below.
  - Getting dragged into the coachee's past – in Conscious Coaching we can choose to explore the past briefly as it can impact on the present and future, but we don't want to get bogged down in minutiae. If this starts to happen, move the coachee on. Thank them for sharing what they've shared, and suggest you now focus on what they want to change.
  - The leader or manager-as-coach letting their own judgements and biases get in the way (see Chapter 7).
  - The leader or manager-as-coach not understanding or managing relationship dynamics (see Chapter 7).

- **On the side of the coachee**
  - Not committing fully to the coaching – if this happens, call it out and if still nothing changes, bring an end to the coaching. Perhaps it's just not the right time for them to engage.
- **On the side of the organization**
  - Forcing people to sign up for coaching – this rarely works, coaching needs to be voluntary.
  - Not having in place a coaching culture which empowers people to try out new behaviours.

Let's look at some of these.

## Working with emotions

Many people who are new to coaching fear others expressing strong emotions. How can you maintain professional separation and maintain focus on the other's needs whilst being empathetic and offering support? What if someone cries or you get upset when faced with strong emotions?

Many coaching clients cry. Tears, or other expressions of emotion, can signal release, a shift of energy, which is good news and usually means you're on to something important.

Mindfulness practice helps us build our capacity to not only be more compassionate and empathetic, but at the same time to stay calm and manage our emotions better.

### What to do and what not to do
Don't ignore strong emotions, but don't rush to comfort either. Sit or stand quietly, give the person space, offer a tissue if they're crying, and once the emotion has passed, which it will,

ask gently, 'Would you like to talk about what just happened there?'

It takes practice to identify emotions and feelings. Like thoughts, they can suddenly pop into our awareness and we might not know why or where they've come from, or we might get them confused with thoughts. Sometimes when we're asked how we're feeling, we respond, 'I think . . .' which obviously is a thought.

---

## Try this: Labelling emotions

### 10 Minutes

You will need a notepad.

### Objectives

- Improving your or the coachee's ability to detect and identify emotions
- Building familiarity with the link between emotions, thoughts and bodily sensations
- Increasing self-awareness and the ability to self-manage

- **Step 1**
  Use the practice outlined on page 8, 'Getting mindful', to get into an intentioned mindset for the exercise.
- **Step 2**
  Noticing any emotions that present themselves (they may be linked to bodily sensations and thoughts, but focus on the emotions) – there may be none, one or many. Seeing if you can label them.

## Identifying emotions

A study of self-reported emotional experiences identified twenty-seven categories,[1] but feel free to invent your own! The categories were:

| | | |
|---|---|---|
| admiration | confusion | joy |
| adoration | craving | nostalgia |
| aesthetic appreciation | disgust | romance |
| | empathetic pain | sadness |
| amusement | entrancement | satisfaction |
| anxiety | envy | sexual desire |
| awe | excitement | sympathy |
| awkwardness | fear | triumph |
| boredom | horror | |
| calmness | interest | |

There may be times when someone talks about an issue that resonates with our own experience, and we get 'triggered'. At such times, we can draw on mindfulness within the session to resource ourselves. We do this by kindly acknowledging to ourselves what's coming up for us personally, grounding ourselves by focusing on our breath and the rise and fall of our abdomen, and feeling our feet. Then we can offer support and express empathy without making the session about us. If this doesn't work – say, someone is sharing their grief and we too have recently been bereaved – we may not be the best person for the job at this time. And that is okay. We can without shame refer the person on to someone else who isn't going through the same experience.

# 11 Coaching for Stress and Mental Health Problems

Let's now explore how we can coach others specifically around well-being and for greater resilience to stress-related and mental health problems.

In this chapter you'll learn:

- how to navigate coaching those with mental health issues
- tips and exercises for working on stress and resilience.

## Coaching people with mental health issues

As leaders and managers coaching others, we need to be aware that mental health problems are extremely common and that very often people don't realize they're mentally unwell, and nor do others around them.

One client, Mary, had no previous history of mental illness and was performing very well at work. When she was diagnosed with clinical depression, it came as a shock to her and her work colleagues. But this was the turning point that allowed recovery to take place, and for her to access the benefits of coaching. She believes that the experience means she is not only stronger and more resilient but a better and more supportive leader. She now shares her story in her place of work to encourage others to come forward and get the support they need.

How can we work in coaching to support people who are struggling, helping them manage stress and become resilient?

## Tips for working on stress and resilience

- Start all sessions with a mindfulness practice.
- Don't assume that because someone shares personal information about their health with you that they're necessarily asking for help. If in doubt, ask.
- If stress is identified as a problem, discuss how widespread stress has become and what happens when we become stressed. Try to work out what the individual's own 'stress alarms' are and invite them to engage in the exercises laid out below.
- Share resources on what the science says, with those who are interested.

How do we make the right call as to whether someone is well enough to be coached? For highly experienced coach and coaching supervisor Eve Turner, it's about: 'considering whether the condition means the person we are working with is capable of functioning in the world . . . staying alert to possibilities – not to rule out someone because they have a mental health condition but to understand the context and make a judgment, and that includes on my competence.'[1]

There are a number of books offering more in-depth guidance.[2]

Below are some exercises you can do around this topic.

# Try this: Nourishing and depleting exercise

## 10 Minutes

You will need a notepad for this exercise.

## Objectives

- Identifying what drains us and what gives us energy
- Prompting actions to increase energizing activities and reduce those that deplete us

- **Step 1**
  Divide a piece of paper into two columns. In one column, write the heading 'Nourishing & energizing'. In a second column, write 'Depleting & draining'.
- **Step 2**
  Imagine a typical day, bringing to mind the different activities and tasks you're involved in at work and in your life in general.
- **Step 3**
  In your notepad catalogue these according to whether you find them depleting or nourishing.
- **Step 4**
  Reflect and take action.

  What can you do to ramp up the nourishing aspects and reduce/modify/delegate the more depleting ones?

## Pressing pause

Research indicates it's better to practice mindfulness daily, albeit in short bursts of at least ten minutes, than for long but infrequent periods.[3] In addition to building mindfulness capacities incrementally, short practices are easy to weave into busy working days.

## Try this: SOAR[4]

### 5 Minutes

- **Step 1**
  Softening: by starting this practice with the invitation to soften, you can quickly let go of physical tension, which is often a manifestation of contracting against what you don't want or grasping tightly on to what you don't want to lose.

  Scanning your body for areas of tension – forehead, eyes, jaws, shoulders, abdomen and so on – and as you go through, gently inviting these to soften and release, feeling the softening spread through your body, softening any tightness too around thoughts, emotions, stories.
- **Step 2**
  Opening: having softened, you can be more open to what is presenting. Tuning into a sense of opening in your body, smiling, widening your shoulders, opening your arms, your hands, widening your stance. With openness comes curiosity about whatever has shown up in our inner and outer worlds.
- **Step 3**
  Allowing: moving on to allowing whatever is here to be here, whatever is to be, meeting your experience with a spirit of acceptance, or kindness. Dropping any urge to judge or to criticize.

- **Step 4**
  Recharging: most of us have our own sense of what nourishes, nurtures and energizes us.

  Here tuning in to whatever personally recharges you. Feeling your feet on the ground, perhaps imagining you're a tree with roots going into the rich fertile earth; tuning into God, some other deity or general sense of the divine, or to nature, the vision or memory of beautiful surroundings, the source of life.

- **Step 5**
  Bringing this little practice to a close, taking this sense of a softer, more open, allowing and resourced stance into whatever you do next.

## CASE STUDY

### Jonah's story

Jonah was a hugely bright and creative leader working in the media. He loved his job but was feeling overwhelmed by the constant pressures at work and wanted to explore how he could be more resilient, learning some techniques he could bring in on a day-to-day basis.

He flew into the coaching sessions like a whirlwind. He spoke quickly and almost breathlessly, with a flurry of ideas emerging from his mouth. As his coach, I was entranced by his conceptual brilliance, whilst impacted by his 'raciness' – I could feel myself speeding up as I talked, a knot in my stomach, and an urge to lean far forward, which is what he was doing.

After sharing what was going on for me – which resonated with him – we practised some mindful belly breathing (see below). Like so many of us, Jonah very much lived in his head and had forgotten how to breathe 'properly'. In the coaching we explored how he could choose to take a few conscious deep breaths to help him calm down when he could hear himself gabbling and could feel unpleasant physical symptoms. He learnt how to 'belly breathe'.

---

When we get stressed, our breathing becomes shallower. When we practise mindfulness, our breaths naturally become deeper and slower, and we stimulate the vagus nerve, one of the most important nerves in the body. It helps to regulate the heart rate, blood pressure, sweating, digestion and speaking. The longest nerve of the autonomic nervous system (ANS), it is intimately connected to the parasympathetic branch of the ANS and thus plays a big role in regulating stress.

---

## Try this: Belly breathing

### 5 Minutes

- **Step 1**
Use the practice outlined on page 8, 'Getting mindful', to get into an intentioned mindset for the exercise.
- **Step 2**
Placing your hand on your abdomen to help you connect with your body. Taking three consciously deep breaths, expanding your abdomen as you breathe in. Noticing what happens to the quality of your breathing.

## Developing compassion and kindness

I outlined earlier the benefits, which include greater resilience, of actively supporting coachees to be kinder and more compassionate towards themselves, and I shared some techniques for developing compassion and kindness. Introducing the key concepts and tools for developing compassion to those who are struggling can be immensely helpful.

One thing to watch out for: if a coachee is highly self-critical, tread gently. Don't go straight in with the loving kindness meditation – they will need time to build up to that, if at all. The compassion-focused imagery exercise and the self-compassion break are gentle ways in.

# Afterword: Is the Future Teal?

> 'The best way to predict the future is to create it.'
> – Peter Drucker

As I write this, our children and others are taking to the streets all over the world to protest that not enough is being done to tackle climate change. It's just one example of the self-responsibility the late Sir John Whitmore talked about in relation to a coaching style being more widely needed and adopted. Sir John used to say he longed for a time when the word coaching is no longer in use because a coaching style has just become part of how things are done.

In an interview he said, 'Finally we're coming to a point where people will take on responsibility for themselves and not rely on a hierarchy . . . the primary product of coaching is self-responsibility. Coaching grew up to meet this need. We've got to get to the stage of self-responsibility for everyone. When that happens, the word coaching will disappear.'[1]

Maybe that will happen or maybe we'll find a new word, just like we found the word coaching. However, one thing's for sure: so much of what coaching seeks to develop, such as self-awareness and self-responsibility, will become even more important as we move forward in these uncertain times. Times when job roles will disappear completely and new ones emerge, when technology will have impacts most of us can't even imagine, when devastation from climate change will, sadly, grow and again have impacts unimaginable for many of us.

As individual human beings, we evolve in stages – as research by psychologists, such as Abraham Maslow, and academics including Robert Kegan, Susanne Cook-Greuter and Bill Torbert has highlighted. Humanity as a whole evolves in stages too, in big leaps. It's happened before, such as in the Enlightenment – the 'Age of Reason' – and it's happening again. Each new stage of development, of consciousness, has brought wide-sweeping changes in society, the economy, power structures and so on. The organizations we invent are a product of the worldview that prevails at each time. In his hugely influential book, Frederic Laloux describes the next stage in human evolution as 'Evolutionary-Teal',[2] which he sees as marked by the following traits.

- Taming the fears of the ego
- Shifting to an internal compass of inner rightness
- Embracing life as a journey of personal and collective unfolding towards our true nature
- Embracing the shift from a deficit- to a strengths-based paradigm (where as humans we're potential waiting to unfold)
- Dealing gracefully with adversity
- Wisdom beyond rationality
- Striving for wholeness – in relation to others, and with life and nature

Sounds pretty good to me, and precisely what's required in these challenging times.

There's something too about courage. Zen Buddhist, highly

experienced corporate coach and co-founder of Relume, Claire Breeze says that when she supervises coaches, she asks them, 'When the chips are down, who are you really working for?' She says:

> Many say they work fundamentally for the individual. Now I don't make that wrong, I think that's very laudable. However, if we're unconsciously erring on the side of the individual and not taking enough responsibility for the state of the companies we're working in, I think paradoxically we might be propping up people and systems that should not necessarily be sustained. Coaching can be a radical practice of empowerment. At our best, as coaches, we're a force for radical change and good. At our worst, we prop up complacent systems.[3]

Laloux recounts how he was asked by Ricardo Semler, author of *Maverick!*, why things should be any different now. After all, there's been hope before and nothing really changed (in the workplace). We haven't seen widespread adoption of the pioneering self-management practices fostered in Semler's company and shared in *Maverick!*. But, like Laloux, I believe wholeheartedly that it's time for change. And the call for and the commitment to developing and spreading coaching, mindfulness and compassion is part of this.

There's something in the air. It smells like hope.

# Acknowledgements

I'm deeply grateful to all my wonderful clients, and to the many kind souls who supported me in the researching and writing of this book, giving their time to coach me (Mark McMordie), read through the book and offer feedback (Raymond and Dean Freeman) and to share their stories and discuss the topics emerging, including Aboodi Shabi, Alison Carter, Ben Van Den Assem, Carroll Macey, Catherine Midgley, Iñigo Castillo, Georgios Poularas, Matthew Runeckles, Rachel Lilley, Sophie Turner and Ram Ramanathan. I wish I could have included all of your pearls of wisdom!

Thanks to Penguin's Martina O'Sullivan for believing in me – such a pleasure to work with you again. And to Celia Buzak from Penguin, who did a remarkable job editing and helping me put the book together.

Special thanks to all my mindfulness teachers, including Thich Nhat Hanh (Thay) and Bodhin, and my coaching teachers, including Carol Wilson, Caroline Horner, Eunice Aquilina, Sir John Whitmore, and to Nancy Kline who inspired me to train as a coach.

# Appendix 1: Tips for Picking a Coach

- **Do you feel you can trust them?** A strong healthy relationship is vital.
- **Are they accredited?** Leading professional coaching bodies joined forces with *Coaching at Work* magazine to compile comparison tables for some of the different bodies' accreditation schemes.[1]
- **Do they have professional indemnity insurance?** It's unlikely that it'll be needed but best to be safe, and it shows they're a professional.
- **Do they sign up to an ethical code?** This may include the Global Code of Ethics for those working within coaching, mentoring and supervision, created by two leading professional coaching bodies – the Association for Coaching and the European Mentoring & Coaching Council. The code aligns with the content and requirements set out in the Professional Charter for Coaching and Mentoring, drafted in accordance with European law and registered on the European Union database of self-regulation initiatives in Europe. Additional signatories include the Association for Professional Executive Coaching and Supervision, Associazione Italiana Coach Professionisti, International Mentoring Institute, Mentoring Institute,

University of New Mexico.[2] Another leading coaching body, the International Coach Federation, has its own equally valid code of ethics.[3]

- **Do they get regular coaching supervision?**
- **Can they articulate their particular approach and what informs this?**
- **If you're choosing a team coach, ask in addition:**
  - **Have they received training as a team coach?**
  - **Whether they've done 'inner work'** such as coach training with strong psychological underpinnings, personal therapy and mindfulness, so they are equipped to deal with complex and challenging team/group dynamics.
  - **Whether they receive team coaching supervision**, and how they surface and work with the wider systemic influences and patterns that impact on teams' purposes and functioning.

## Tips for choosing a mindfulness coach/teacher

- **Do they have a regular mindfulness practice?**
- **Do they go on retreat?**
- **Have they trained as a mindfulness teacher?**
- **If not, what qualifies them to work with mindfulness?**

The UK Mindfulness Network has published Good Practice Guidelines for mindfulness teachers. They're rigorous and don't necessarily apply to a coach who works with mindfulness but doesn't teach it, but they offer pointers.[4]

It's a great idea to learn mindfulness in a group; you'll learn more and you'll be supported in embedding new habits.

Programmes available in lots of countries include eight-week Mindfulness-Based Stress Reduction or Mindfulness-Based Cognitive Therapy programmes (anyone can attend these, you don't have to be stressed or mentally unwell) or variations on these. There are also books available which take the reader through versions of these programmes, such as Mark Williams and Danny Penman's *Mindfulness: A practical guide to finding peace in a frantic world*. And there are heaps of programmes on developing compassion too, such as those offered by Kristin Neff and Christopher Germer.[5]

# Appendix 2: Coaching Programme Planning

## Frequently asked questions

Below are some frequently asked questions (FAQs) to help you plan a programme of one-to-one coaching sessions

- **How many?**
  Even a sole coaching conversation can have a huge impact, but habits take time to change. Typically, a coaching programme will consist of anything from three to twelve sessions, but most commonly it will be six.
- **How often?**
  Allow at least a week and up to a month between each session.
- **Does coaching have to be optional?**
  Yes. Gone are the days when coaching was primarily used in the workplace as a remedial tool. For coaching to really work, the person being coached has to be on board.
- **Who needs to know?**
  It depends. You may want to involve other parties in drawing up the coaching agreement. Third-party agreements are common in workplace coaching and typically involve the person who has agreed to be

coached, the person coaching them (line manager, HR, etc.) and another party (could be whoever the line manager reports to).

- **Initial goal setting/identifying overarching purpose**

  Whilst I've said elsewhere that Conscious Coaching acknowledges that goal setting can be overly strict and inappropriate at times, this doesn't mean embarking upon coaching at work with no idea of where you're going. You'll need to discuss and agree with the person being coached, and possibly another party, what the coaching is for. What are the overall aims – career development, on-boarding for a new role, building resilience, helping them be more emotionally intelligent, and so on? In the first session, you can explore further what the coaching will address.

- **Where and how?**

  If you're doing the coaching face-to-face, preferably find somewhere peaceful where you won't be disturbed, maybe even getting away from the office – you could even go for a walk with the person you're coaching in a local park. Otherwise, a quiet space somewhere in the workplace.

  Or you could do the coaching online, via Skype or Zoom, for example. Or even by phone. What you may lose in terms of not seeing the person's body language, they may gain from being better able to focus. You could even coach someone via email – although this wouldn't necessarily be in real time. It works well if you're in different geographical locations, and gives both of you time to reflect before you respond.

  A blend of face-to-face and online can work well.

- **How long should each session be?**
Anything between half an hour and an hour and a half works well.

- **How do I manage the time?**
You'll get better at doing so with practice. I tend to put a clock where I can easily see it, without breaking rapport with my client, to look at the time. If you find you've suddenly got lots of time to spare, just ask the other person what they would like to work on. Sometimes, coaching conversations naturally come to a close and it's okay to just stop.

- **How do we evaluate the coaching?**
In some organizations, there is such belief that coaching works that they don't bother to evaluate, or instead of 'return on investment', they think in terms of 'return on expectations'.

  One simple way to evaluate is to compare where the person was at the beginning of the coaching with where they ended up (be careful not to be too attached to them achieving the initial goals identified, they *will* shift), and to gather their comments on benefits reaped from the process – for themselves, their team and the organization.

  Other measures before and after coaching include 360-degree feedback surveys (particularly if there are multiple coaching assignments happening); gathering hard data on absenteeism and staff retention, for example; measuring the bottom line performance.

# Appendix 3: Planning Your Coaching Sessions

Below is a suggested plan for a series of six one-hour coaching sessions, plus a 'chemistry meeting'.

## The chemistry meeting

Before embarking upon coaching, I suggest you first have a chat in person or online. In this initial conversation, address and explore the following.

- **What does the person understand by coaching?**
  Often people get it mixed up with mentoring. You'll need to be able to explain the differences, which I outlined earlier.
- **What do they want from coaching?**
  They may want to work on something you can't or don't want to work on, or for which someone else would be better placed to help them. Don't get into details but do explore what they generally want to work on.
- **How will you work together, and will this suit you both?**
  They may want more sessions than you've time to offer, or they may want to meet in person each time, which

you can't do. They may want someone who is very challenging and forceful to work with, and you may not want to work like that. On the other hand, it can be a great stretch and good for learning for either party to work with someone adopting a style that's outside their comfort zone. Explore and see if you can agree. If you're planning to implement Conscious Coaching, incorporating mindfulness and compassion into how you work, you have a choice to tell them upfront, or offer it as you go along.

## Session 1: The introductory session

In this session, you go into what the coaching will address in much more detail.

The order of the session is: set the scene; explore the reality; prioritize goals/outcomes/intentions/purpose; agree which ones to focus on; closure and next steps.

### 1  Set the scene

Agree how long the session will be.

Switch off mobiles.

Suggest doing a very brief mindfulness practice together, explain why (help you both get more focused and grounded so you can work better together).

Explain what the purpose is of this first session: exploring what's going on currently and agreeing what the overarching purpose and the hoped-for outcomes are by the end of the coaching.

Reassure them that everything that takes place is confidential.

Let them know that they can ask questions at
any time.

**2 Set the outcome**

What do they want to achieve in this session?

**3 Explore briefly what's currently going on**

Invite them to share what's happening in their work
(and life – we bring our lives into work and vice versa).

Make a list of things they want to focus on and
change.

**4 Prioritize together the areas they'd like to focus on**

Read back the initial list to them. What do they want to
let go of and what needs to stay? Ask them to make a list
of these.

Help them identify the top three using the EXACT
model outlined earlier – **E**xplicit, e**X**citing, **A**ssessable,
**C**hallenging, **T**ime-framed (over the next three to six
months). Or you could use GROW, if you prefer. You
could ask them to rate where they are now in relation to
those outcomes in percentage terms (with 100 per cent
signalling total achievement/perfection).

You may return from time to time to some of the
other items. Thanks to the clarity and energy from this
session, the person will probably go off and address
them anyway. Or other items will come up.

**5 Closure and next steps**

Express your appreciation: 'Thank you for being so
honest, I admire your commitment to this process, is
there anything you'd like to say as we close?' Give the
person any worksheets or tools you'd like them to work
on between now and the next session. Agree when
you're next meeting.

# Subsequent sessions (2 to 5)

1  **Set the scene**
   Revisit previous goals/outcomes, explore actions and
   create new ones. Mindfulness practice.
2  **Quick check-in**
   Revisit goals/outcomes – how have they been getting on
   in terms of actions?
3  **Agree what they want to achieve in this session**
   For example, 'I want to get some movement towards
   my goal of . . . ' Encourage them to express their aim
   positively.
4  **Explore**
   Use the time to explore in ways you think will help them
   most with what they're focusing on, trying out the many
   tools and techniques offered in this book.
5  **Set new next steps**
6  **Closure**

## Important elements
Every few sessions:

- Review how far the person has come
- Ask for feedback on your coaching and how the
  coaching process is working out for them. What is
  working well? What is not working so well?
- Expect goals and outcomes to shift. Use the 'four-eyed'
  model as an alternative to EXACT and GROW.

# Final session

1 **Set the scene:** reviewing intentions/goals/purpose/ outcomes and celebrating how far the person has come.
2 **Revisit:** the intentions/goals/purpose/outcomes.
3 **Agree:** what to work on in this final session.
4 **Review the whole series of coaching sessions:** highlighting any key takeaways and learnings. Ask questions like: 'What was your biggest learning?' 'What have you learnt about yourself and others?' 'What are the key benefits for yourself, the team and the organization?' (Keep a note of their responses with their permission; anonymous comments can be used to justify resources allocated to coaching.) You could ask them to complete a self-report evaluation questionnaire after the coaching. If you invited them to rate where they were with goals, you could ask them to give percentages for where they are now after the coaching: 'As a percentage, how close are you to achieving what you set out to achieve?'
   Ask for feedback on your coaching: 'What did you like best about how you were coached?' 'What would you have liked to have been done differently?'
5 **Closure on the session and the whole series:** Acknowledge there may be certain emotions, such as sadness or relief that the programme has come to an end.

# Endnotes

## Introduction

1　Lord Dennis Stevenson and Paul Farmer, 'Thriving at Work: a review of mental health and employers', independent review published 26 October 2017.

2　Mental Health America, 2017.

3　World Economic Forum, 'The Future of Jobs Report 2018', published 17 September 2018.

4　And incidentally, VUCA means 'to wake up' in the Zulu language: Joel and Michelle Levey, http://www.wisdomatwork.com/about/thriving-in-vuca-times/ (accessed April 2019).

5　Larry Alton, 'How Millennials Are Reshaping What's Important In Corporate Culture', *Forbes*, 20 June 2017.

6　Hieker, C. and Topale, H., 2019, 'Millennials at work', *Coaching at Work* 14(1), 43–5.

7　Grant, A. and Hartley, M., 2013, 'Developing the leader as coach: Insights, strategies and tips for embedding coaching skills in the workplace', *Coaching: An International Journal of Theory, Research and Practice*, 6, 102–15.

8　Reitz et al, *The Mindful Leader: Developing the capacity for resilience and collaboration in complex times through mindfulness practice*, Hult Research/Ashridge Executive Education, 2016.

## 1. Starting the Journey

1　ICF website, https://www.icfcoachingworks.com/ (accessed December 2018).

2　Ridler & Co, 'The 6th Ridler Report', published in 2016.

3   Jon Kabat-Zinn, author of *Wherever You Go, There You Are: Mindfulness meditation for everyday life* (Piatkus, 1994) and founder of the Stress Reduction Clinic at the University of Massachusetts.

4   Mental Health Foundation, 'Be Mindful Report', published in 2010, p. 5.

5   https://themindfulnessinitiative.org.uk/about-mindfulness/ what-is-it (accessed April 2019).

6   Ellen Langer, 2000, 'Mindful Learning', *Current Directions in Psychological Science*, 9(6), 220.

7   When guiding mindfulness exercises, it's best practice to use the present participle rather than the imperative – *noticing* rather than *notice*, and so on – as it's more inviting, and reflects the ongoing and present-focused nature of mindfulness.

8   The Triangle of Awareness was created by some teachers at the University of Massachusetts Medical School's Center for Mindfulness. See Donald McCown, Diane Reibel and Marc Micozzi, *Teaching Mindfulness: A Practical Guide for Clinicians and Educators*, Springer, 2011.

9   https://compassionatemind.co.uk/about-us (accessed April 2019).

10  Tim Anstiss, 2017, 'Compassion at Work', *The IJMC*, pilot issue (1), 14–16.

11  https://www.roffeypark.com/compassion-at-work-index/ (accessed April 2019).

## 2. The Research

1   ILM, 2018 report, 'Cracking coaching: Five ways to make an impact at work', p. 2.

2   Green, L. S., Oades, L. G. and Grant, A. M., 2006, 'Cognitive-behavioural, solution-focused life coaching: Enhancing goal striving, well-being and hope', *Journal of Positive Psychology*, 1(3), 142–9.

3   Hicks, B., Carter, A. and Sinclair, A., *Impact of coaching on employee well-being, engagement and job satisfaction*, Institute of Employment Studies, 2014.

4   Grant, A. M. and O'Connor, S. A. 'Executive Coaching in Times of Organizational Change', in Liz Hall (ed.), *Coaching in Times of Crisis and Transformation*, Kogan Page, 2015, pp. 121–43.

5 Katherine Ashby and Michelle Mahdon, *Why do employees come to work when ill? An investigation into sickness presence in the workplace*, The Work Foundation, 2010.

6 Kivimäki et al, 2015, 'Long working hours and risk of coronary heart disease and stroke: A systematic review and meta-analysis of published and unpublished data for 603,838 individuals', *The Lancet*, 386 (10005), 1739–46.

7 UK charity Business in the Community (BITC)'s 2016 'National Employee Mental Well-being' poll of more than 20,000 people.

8 Walsh, R. and Shapiro, S. L., 2006, 'The meeting of meditative disciplines and Western psychology: A mutually enriching dialogue', *American Psychologist*, 61, 227–39.

9 Spence, G. B., Cavanagh, M. and Grant, A, 2008, 'The integration of mindfulness training and health coaching: An exploratory study', *Coaching: An international journal of theory, research and practice*, 1(2), 1–19.

10 Kristin Neff, 'The Science of Self-Compassion', in Christopher Germer and Ronald Siegel (eds), *Compassion and Wisdom in Psychotherapy*, Guilford Press, 2012, pp. 79–92.

11 Sbarra, D. A., Smith, H. L. and Mehl, M. R., 2012, 'When leaving your ex, love yourself: Observational ratings of self-compassion predict the course of emotional recovery following marital separation', *Psychological Science*, 23(3), 261–9.

12 Neff, K. D., Rude, S. S. and Kirkpatrick, K., 2007, 'An examination of self-compassion in relation to positive psychological functioning and personality traits', *Journal of Research in Personality*, 41, 908–16.

13 Dutton, J. E., Lilius, J. M. and Kanov, J., 'The transformative potential of compassion at work', in Piderit, S. K., Cooperider, D. L. and Fry, R. E. (eds), *Handbook of Transformative Cooperation: New designs and dynamics*, Stanford University Press, 2007, pp. 107–26.

14 Bronwyn Fryer, 'The Rise of Compassionate Management (Finally)', *Harvard Business Review*, 18 September 2013.

15 https://vimeo.com/55527208 (accessed May 2019).

16 Abraham, R., 'Emotional intelligence in the workplace: A review and synthesis', in Schulze, R. and Roberts, R. D. (eds), *Emotional*

*Intelligence: An International Handbook*, Hogrefe & Huber, 2005, pp. 255–70.

17 Byrne, J. C., 2004, 'The role of emotional intelligence in predicting leadership and related work behavior', doctoral dissertation, Stevens Institute of Technology.

18 Stubbs, E. C., 2005, 'Emotional intelligence competencies in the team and team leader: A multi-level examination of the impact of emotional intelligence on group performance', doctoral dissertation, Case Western Reserve University.

19 Chapman, M., 'Emotional Intelligence and Coaching: An Exploratory Study', in Cavanagh, M., Grant, A. M. and Kemp, T. (eds), *Evidence-based coaching 1: Theory, research and practice from the behavioural sciences*, Australian Academic Press, 2005, pp. 183–92.

20 Grant, A. M., 2007, 'Enhancing coaching skills and emotional intelligence through training', *Industrial and Commercial Training*, 39(5), 257–66.

21 Hughes S., 2018, 'How could coaching help executives handle workplace conflict?', action research study, unpublished MA dissertation, Oxford Brookes University.

22 Dijkstra, M., Beersma, B. and Cornelissen, R. A., 2012, 'The emergence of the Activity Reduces Conflict Associated Strain (ARCAS) model: A test of a conditional mediation model of workplace conflict and employee strain', *Journal of Occupational Health Psychology*, 17(3), p. 365.

23 Richard Boyatzis and Annie McKee, *Resonant leadership: Renewing yourself and connecting with others through mindfulness, hope, and compassion*, Harvard Business Press, 2005.

24 Creswell, J. D., Way, B. M., Eisenberger, N. I. and Lieberman, M. D., 2007, 'Neural correlates of dispositional mindfulness during affect labelling', *Psychosomatic medicine*, 69(6), 560–65.

25 Casey, P., Burke, K. and Leben, S., 2013, 'Minding the court: Enhancing the decision-making process', *International Journal for Court Administration*, 5, 45–54.

26 Reb, J., Narayanan, J. and Chaturvedi, S., 2012, 'Leading mindfully: Two studies on the influence of supervisor trait mindfulness on employee wellbeing and performance', *Mindfulness*, 5(1), 36–45.

27 Dutton et al, 'The transformative potential of compassion'.

28 Grant, A. M., Dutton, J. E. and Rosso, B. D., 2017, 'Giving commitment: Employee support programs and the prosocial sensemaking process', *Academy of Management Journal*, 51(5), 898–918.

29 Neff et al, 'An examination of self-compassion'.

30 Neff, K. D. and Beretvas, S. N., 2013, 'The role of self-compassion in romantic relationships', *Self and Identity*, 12(1), 78–98.

31 Dutton et al, 'The transformative potential of compassion'.

32 ILM, 'Cracking coaching'.

33 David Clutterbuck, *Coaching the Team at Work*, Nicholas Brealey, 2007.

34 Ruth Wageman, Debra Nunes, James Burruss and Richard Hackman, *Senior leadership teams: What it takes to make them great*, Harvard Business Review Press, 2008.

35 Brightstone, 2019, 'Serving Up Success with Legal & General', https://www.brightstone.co.uk/client-success-stories/serving-success-legal-general/ (accessed April 2019).

36 Hall, L., 2019, 'Legal & General initiative boosts staff progress', *Coaching at Work*, 14 (1), 8.

37 Global '2017 ICF Global Consumer Awareness Study'. It was carried out by PwC Research, and drew 27,134 responses from 30 countries.

38 Reb, J., Narayanan, J. and Ho, Z. W., 2013, 'Mindfulness at work: Antecedents and consequences of employee awareness and absent-mindedness', *Mindfulness*, 6(1), 111–22.

39 Greenberg, J., Reiner, K. and Meiran, N., 2012, ' "Mind the trap": Mindfulness practice reduces cognitive rigidity', *PLOS ONE*, 7(5), e36206.

40 Kirk, U., Downar, J. and Montague, P. R., 2011, 'Interoception drives increased rational decision-making in meditators playing the ultimatum game', *Frontiers in Neuroscience*, 5, 49.

41 Ostafin, B. and Kassman, K., 2012, 'Stepping out of history: Mindfulness improves problem solving', *Consciousness and Cognition*, 21(2), 1031–6.

42 Zabelina, D. L. and Robinson, M. D., 2010, 'Don't be so hard on yourself: Self-compassion facilitates creative originality among

self-judgmental individuals', *Creativity Research Journal*, 22(3), 288–93.

43 Melwani, S., Mueller, J. S. and Overbeck, J. R., 2012, 'Looking down: The influence of contempt and compassion on emergent leadership categorizations', *Journal of Applied Psychology*, 97(6), 1171.

44 Grant et al, 'Giving commitment'.

45 Lilius et al, 2008, 'The contours and consequences of compassion at work', *Journal of Organizational Behavior*, 29(2), 193–218.

46 Goodwin, J., 2017, 'Boots: Unlocking potential', *Coaching at Work*, 12(6), 31–33.

47 MacKie, D., 2014, 'The effectiveness of strength-based executive coaching in enhancing full range leadership development: A controlled study', *Consulting Psychology Journal: Practice and Research*, 66(2), 118.

48 Cerni, T., Curtis, G. J. and Colmar, S. H., 2010, 'Executive coaching can enhance transformational leadership', *International Coaching Psychology Review*, 5, 81–4.

49 Grant, A. M., Green, S. L. and Rynsaardt, J., 2010, 'Developmental coaching for high school teachers: Executive coaching goes to school', *Consulting Psychology Journal: Practice and Research*, 62(3), 151–68.

50 Erik de Haan and Anthony Kasozi, 'Leaders in Crisis: Attending to the Shadow Side', in Liz Hall (ed.), *Coaching in Times of Crisis and Transformation*, Kogan Page, 2015, pp. 144–71.

51 Simon Cavicchia and Maria Gilbert, *The Theory and Practice of Relational Coaching: Complexity, Paradox and Integration*, Routledge, 2018.

52 Amel, E. L., Manning, C. M. and Scott, B. A., 2009, 'Mindfulness and sustainable behavior: Pondering attention and awareness as means for increasing green behavior', *Ecopsychology*, 1(1), 14–25.

53 Shapiro, S. L., Jazaieri, H. and Goldin, P. R., 2012, 'Mindfulness-based stress reduction effects on moral reasoning and decision making', *The Journal of Positive Psychology*, 7(6), 504–15.

54 Ericson, T., Kjønstad, B. G. and Barstad, A., 2014, 'Mindfulness and sustainability', *Ecological Economics*, 104, 73–9.

55 Reitz et al, *The Mindful Leader: Developing the capacity for resilience and collaboration in complex times through mindfulness practice*, Hult Research/Ashridge Executive Education, 2016.

56 Personal interview, 1 December 2018.

57 Grant and O'Connor, 'Executive Coaching'.

58 International Coach Federation and Human Capital Institute, *Building a Coaching Culture for Change Management*, 2018.

59 ILM, 'Cracking coaching'.

60 According to the ICF/HCI report, which surveyed more than 430 participants, including HR, L&D and talent management professionals, internal coach practitioners and managers.

61 ILM, 'Cracking coaching'.

62 Grant and O'Connor, 'Executive Coaching'.

63 Hall, L., 2014, 'Good news', *Coaching at Work*, 9(2), 22–6.

## 3. Understanding Yourself and Others

1 The Ancient Greek philosopher has been frequently quoted by, among others, Will Durant in *The Story of Philosophy* (first edition 1926), Simon and Schuster, 1961.

2 Maguire et al, 2000, 'Navigation-related structural change in the hippocampi of taxi drivers', *PNAS*, 97(8), 4398–4403.

3 Jack et al, 2013, 'Visioning in the brain: an fMRI study of inspirational coaching and mentoring', *Social neuroscience*, 8(4), 369–84.

4 Hölzel et al, 2011, 'Mindfulness practice leads to increases in regional brain gray matter density', *Psychiatry Research: Neuroimaging*, 191(1), 36–43.

5 Lazar et al, 2005, 'Meditation experience is associated with increased cortical thickness', *Neuroreport*, 16(17), 1893.

6 Jack et al, 'Visioning in the brain'.

7 Gershon, M. D., 1999, 'The enteric nervous system: A second brain', *Hospital Practice*, 34(7), 31–52.

8 McCraty, R., Atkinson, M. and Bradley, R. T., 2004, 'Electrophysiological evidence of intuition: Part 1. The surprising role of the heart', *The Journal of Alternative & Complementary Medicine*, 10(1), 133–43; 'Part 2. A system-wide process?' *JACM*, 10(2), 325–36.

9   Mark Williams and Danny Penman, *Mindfulness: A practical guide to finding peace in a frantic world*, Hachette, 2011, p. 20.

10  The Body Scan is the second mindfulness practice that participants on the standard Mindfulness Based Stress Reduction or Mindfulness Based Cognitive Therapy programmes are invited to do.

11  Antonio Damasio, *The Strange Order of Things: Life, Feeling, and the Making of Cultures*, Pantheon Books, 2018.

12  Liz Fosslien and Mollie West Duffy, *No Hard Feelings*, Portfolio/Penguin, 2019.

13  Fredrickson, B. L., 1998, 'What good are positive emotions?' *Review of General Psychology*, 2, 300–19.

14  Fredrickson, B. L. and Cohn, M. A., 'Positive emotions' in Lewis, M., Haviland-Jones, J. M. and Barrett, L. F. (eds), *Handbook of Emotions* (3rd edition), Guilford Press, 2010, pp. 777–96.

15  The term 'psychological safety' was used by Amy Edmondson, the Novartis Professor of Leadership and Management at the Harvard Business School, in her 1999 paper, 'Psychological Safety and Learning Behavior in Work Teams', *Administrative Science Quarterly*, 44(2), 350–83. Her research suggested the most cohesive teams were those making the most mistakes – but she realized this was just because they were more willing and able to talk about their errors.

16  Zindel Segal, 'The Difference Between "Being" and "Doing"', *Mindful*, 27 October 2016.

17  Friedman, R. S. and Forster, J., 2001, 'The Effects of Promotion and Prevention Cues on Creativity', *Journal of Personality and Social Psychology*, 81(6), 1001–13.

## 4. Starting from the Inside Out: Coaching Ourselves

1   Rachel Ellison, 'Self-coaching', in Liz Hall (ed.), *Coaching in Times of Crisis and Transformation*, Kogan Page, 2015, pp. 222–45.

## 5. Coaching One-to-One: Laying the Foundations

1   Jon Kabat-Zinn, *Wherever You Go, There You Are: Mindfulness meditation in everyday life*, Hyperion, 2004.

2   See Shunryu Suzuki, *Zen Mind, Beginner's mind* (Shambhala Publications, 2005) for informal talks on Zen meditation and practice.

3   Some of us will have tried the Raisin Meditation, which involves eating a raisin mindfully, engaging all our senses, approaching the raisin as if for the first time, with the mind of a beginner. Engaging our beginner's mind can bring back joy and wonder, as we can stop taking people and things for granted.

4   Carol Dweck, *Mindset: The new psychology of success*, Random House, 2008.

5   Beisser, A., 'The paradoxical theory of change', in Fagan, J. and Shepherd, I. L. (eds), *Gestalt Therapy Now*, Harper & Row, 1970, pp. 77–80.

6   Gestalt is an existential/experiential psychotherapeutic approach developed by Fritz Perls (1893–1970) that emphasizes personal responsibility, and focuses on the individual's experience in the present moment.

7   Wood, A. M., Joseph, S. and Maltby, J., 2008, 'Gratitude uniquely predicts satisfaction with life: Incremental validity above the domains and facets of the five factor model', *Personality and Individual Differences*, 45 (1), 49–54.

8   Algoe, S. B., Haidt, J. and Gable, S. L., 2008, 'Beyond reciprocity: Gratitude and relationships in everyday life', *Emotion*, 8(3), 425.

9   Algoe, S. B., Gable, S. L. and Maisel, N. C., 2010, 'It's the little things: Everyday gratitude as a booster shot for romantic relationships', *Personal relationships*, 17(2), 217–33.

10  Reynold Feldman and Cynthia Voelke (eds), *A World Treasury of Folk Wisdom*, HarperCollins, 1992.

11  Brené Brown, *Daring Greatly: How the courage to be vulnerable transforms the way we live, love, parent, and lead*, Penguin, 2015, p. 2.

12  The ICF's code of ethics: https://coachfederation.org/code-of-ethics. The Global Code of Ethics, which has signatories including the Association for Coaching and the European Mentoring & Coaching Council: https://www.globalcodeofethics.org/.

## 6. Coaching One-to-One: Building Rapport

1   Erik de Haan, *Relational Coaching: Journeys towards mastering one-to-one learning,* John Wiley & Sons, 2008.

2   Visser, M., 2010, 'Relating in executive coaching: a behavioural systems approach', *Journal of Management Development*, 29(10), 891–901.

3   McEvoy et al, 2013, 'Empathic curiosity: resolving goal conflicts that generate emotional distress', *Journal of Psychiatric and Mental Health Nursing*, 20(3), 273–78.

4   Kouzakova et al, 2010, 'A stranger's cold shoulder makes the heart grow fonder: Why not being mimicked by a stranger enhances longstanding relationship evaluations', *Social Psychological and Personality Science*, 1(1), 87–93.

5   Clarissa Pinkola Estés, *Women Who Run with the Wolves: Contacting the power of the wild woman*, Random House, 1996.

6   Cited in Frederic Laloux, *Reinventing Organizations: A guide to creating organizations inspired by the next stage of human consciousness*, Nelson Parker, 2014.

## 7. Coaching One-to-One: Facilitating Learning and Results

1   Liz Hall, *Coaching in Times of Crisis and Transformation*, Kogan Page, 2015.

2   Henry David Thoreau and Bob Blaisdell, *Thoreau's Book of Quotations*, Dover Publications, 2000.

3   Oppezzo, M. and Schwartz, D. L., 2014, 'Give your ideas some legs: The positive effect of walking on creative thinking', *Journal of Experimental Psychology: Learning, Memory, and Cognition*, 40(4), 1142–52.

4   Atchley, R. A., Strayer, D. L. and Atchley, P., 2012, 'Creativity in the Wild: Improving creative reasoning through immersion in natural settings', *PLOS ONE*, 7(12), e51474.

5   Berman et al, 2012, 'Interacting with nature improves cognition and affect for individuals with depression', *Journal of Affective Disorders*, 140(3), 300–305.

6   Mackay, G. J. and Neill, J. T., 2010, 'The effect of "green exercise" on state anxiety and the role of exercise duration, intensity, and

greenness: A quasi-experimental study', *Psychology of Sport and Exercise*, 11(3), 238–45.

7  Barton, J., Griffin, M. and Pretty, J., 2012, 'Exercise-, nature- and socially interactive-based initiatives improve mood and self-esteem in the clinical population', *Perspectives in Public Health*, 132(2), 89–96.

8  Thomas, F., 2015, 'The role of natural environments within women's everyday health and wellbeing in Copenhagen, Denmark', *Health & Place*, 35, 187–95.

9  http://isca-network.org/systemic-constellations/what-is-a-constellation (accessed May 2019).

10  Sir John Whitmore, 2017, *Coaching for Performance: The principles and practice of coaching and leadership* (5th edition), Nicholas Brealey, 2017.

11  Hawkins, P. and Turner, E., *Systemic Coaching: Delivering value beyond the individual,* Routledge (in press), 2020.

12  Turner, E., 2019, 'The horns of the dilemma', *Coaching at Work*, 14(2), 48–51.

13  Gardiner Morse, 'Designing a Bias-Free Organization', *Harvard Business Review*, July–August 2016 issue.

14  Karpman, S., 1968, 'Fairy tales and script drama analysis', *Transactional Analysis Bulletin*, 7(26), 39–43; https://www.karpmandramatriangle.com/ (accessed May 2019).

15  Choy, A., 1990, 'The Winner's Triangle', *Transactional Analysis Journal*, 20(1), 40–46.

## 8. Coaching Your Team

1  David Clutterbuck, in Peter Hawkins, *Leadership Team Coaching*, Kogan Page, 2011, p. xii.

2  Peter Hawkins, *Leadership Team Coaching*, p. 10.

3  Laura Delizonna, 'High-Performing Teams Need Psychological Safety. Here's How to Create It', *Harvard Business Review*, 24 August 2017.

4  Paul Gilbert, *The Compassionate Mind*, Constable, 2009.

5  Davidson, R., 'Changing the brain by transforming the mind. The impact of compassion training on the neural systems of emotion',

paper presented at the Mind and Life Institute Conference, Investigating the Mind, Emory University, Atlanta, GA, 2007.

6   Barbara Frederickson, *Love 2.0: Creating Happiness and Health in Moments of Connection*, Penguin, 2013.

7   Paul Ekman, *Emotional Awareness: Overcoming the Obstacles to Psychological Balance and Compassion: A Conversation Between The Dalai Lama and Paul Ekman*, Times Books, 2008, p. 288.

8   Heardman, P., 2017, 'What's love got to do with it?', *Coaching at Work*, 12(3), 42–5.

9   Peter Hawkins and Nick Smith, *Coaching, Mentoring and Organizational Consultancy*, McGraw Hill, 2006.

10  Meredith Belbin and his team identified nine clusters of behaviour, which he called 'team roles'. They are: Resource Investigator (uses their inquisitive nature to bring in ideas); Team Worker (helps the team to gel and identify work required); Coordinator (focuses on team objectives and delegates appropriately); Plant (tends to be highly creative and good at solving problems in unconventional ways); Monitor Evaluator (provides a logical eye); Specialist (brings in-depth knowledge); Shaper (provides drive and keeps up momentum); Implementer (plans and implements a workable strategy), and Completer Finisher (polishes work and scrutinizes for errors). Each has strengths and weaknesses. See https://www.belbin.com/about/belbin-team-roles/.

11  Carter, A., Tobias Mortlock, J. and Spiegelhalter, K., 'Mindfulness in Organisations: Case studies of organisational practice', HR Network Paper 127, IES, published November 2016.

12  Carter, A. and Tobias Mortlock, J., 'Mindfulness in the Military: Improving mental fitness in the UK Armed Forces using next generation team mindfulness training', Report 525, IES and Cranfield University, published May 2019.

## 9. Establishing a Conscious Coaching Culture

1   Thich Nhat Hanh, *Peace is Every Breath: A practice for our busy lives*, Random House, 2011.

2   David Clutterbuck and David Megginson, *Making Coaching Work: Creating a coaching culture*, CIPD Publishing, 2005.

3   Meysam Poorkavoos, 'Compassionate Leadership: What is it and why do organisations need more of it?' research paper, Roffey Park Institute, 2016.

4   Jutta Tobias Mortlock, quoted in The Mindfulness Initiative's report 'Building the case for mindfulness', published October 2016.

5   Karl Weick and Kathleen Sutcliffe, *Managing the Unexpected*, Jossey-Bass, 2007.

6   The Institute of Leadership & Management surveyed 2,000 UK employees in full- and part-time work, in June 2017.

7   http://superhospital.co.uk/why-work-for-us/rewards-and-recognition (accessed May 2019).

8   Nancy Kline, *Time to think: Listening to Ignite the Human Mind*, Hachette, 1999.

9   John Leary-Joyce, *The Fertile Void: Gestalt Coaching at Work*, AOEC Press, 2014.

10   https://www.wmemployers.org.uk/aboutthepool (accessed May 2019).

11   Personal interview, 21 January 2019.

12   Richard Thaler and Cass Sunstein, *Nudge: Improving decisions about health, wealth and happiness*, Penguin, 2009.

13   Barrett, L. F., 2016, 'The theory of constructed emotion', *Social Cognitive and Affective Neuroscience*, 12, 1–23.

14   Baer et al, 2006, 'Using self-report assessment methods to explore facets of mindfulness', *Assessment*, 11(5), 191–206.

## 10. Potential Obstacles to Effective Coaching

1   Cowen, A. S. and Keltner, D, 2017, 'Self-report captures 27 distinct categories of emotion bridged by continuous gradients', *PNAS*, 114(38), E7900–09.

## 11. Coaching for Stress and Mental Health Problems

1   Quoted in Pick, L. and Hall, L., 2017, 'Special report: Coaching in a crisis. Part 1 – Working with mental health issues', *Coaching at Work*, 12(3), 25–31.

2   Andrew Buckley and Carole Buckley, *A Guide to Coaching and Mental Health: The recognition and management of psychological issues*, Routledge, 2012.

3    Reitz et al, *The Mindful Leader: Developing the capacity for resilience and collaboration in complex times through mindfulness practice*, Hult Research/Ashridge Executive Education, 2016.

4    Hall, L., 'Mindful Compassionate Coaching: An Approach Perfect for "VUCA" Times', in English, S., Sabatine, J. and Brownell, P. (eds), *Professional Coaching Principles and Practice*, Springer, 2018, pp. 154–5.

## Afterword: Is the Future Teal?

1    Leni Wildflower, *The Hidden History of Coaching*, Open University Press, 2013.

2    Frederick Laloux, *Reinventing Organizations: A guide to creating organizations inspired by the next stage of human consciousness*, Nelson Parker, 2014.

3    Claire Breeze, 2018, quoted in Hall, L., 'Radical honesty: A profile of Claire Genkai Breeze', *Coaching at Work*, 13(6), 22–5.

## Appendix 1

(All websites accessed May 2019)

1    http://www.coaching-at-work.com/category/accreditation-hub/.

2    www.globalcodeofethics.org.

3    https://coachfederation.org/icf-ethics.

4    https://www.mindfulnessteachersuk.org.uk.

5    https://self-compassion.org/.

# Index

Aberystwyth University 150
acceptance 49
agile leadership 13, 22–7
align5 17
Anstiss, Tim 10
Appletree Answers 16–17
appreciation 52–3
approach system 36, 37
Aristotle 30
art-based coaching 83–4, 88, 127–8
Ashridge Executive Education 23
ask, don't tell 68–9, 113
Association for Coaching 54, 170
authenticity 54
Automotive Fuel Cell Cooperation
    (AFCC) 142
autonomic nervous system(ANS)
    164
avoidance system 36, 37
awareness 8–9

Behavioural Activation System 36, 37
Behavioural Inhibition System 37
being mode 35, 36, 50, 51
Beisser, Arnold 49

belly breathing 164
Bennis, Warren 102
Berne, Eric 98–9
biases 94–7, 155
body, mind and emotions 31–4
Boots Contract Manufacturing
    (BCM) 21–2
brain see mind
breathing 164
Breeze, Claire 168
Broaden and Build 34
Brown, Brené 53–4
Buddhism 6, 45, 49

Castillo, Iñigo 23–5
Cavicchia, Simon 22
change xiii, 49
  – see also organizational change
Choy, Acey 100–101
CID-CLEAR model 118–22
clarifying 64, 116
Clutterbuck, David 103,
    135–6
coaches 41
  – tips for picking 170–71

coaching xiv–xv, 3–4, 13
- and agile leadership 22–7
- and approach system 37
- and emotional intelligence 17–18
- ethical, legal and professional guidelines 55, 170–71
- the future 166–8
- and implementing change 14, 27–9
- and mentoring 5
- and neuroplasticity 31
- organizational culture 135–6
- potential obstacles 155–68
- and productivity 19–21
- and resilience 14–16, 17
- and therapy or counselling 5
- and training 5
- see also Conscious Coaching; one-to-one coaching; team coaching
communication
- one-to-one coaching 61–70
- team coaching 114–17
compassion 3, 6, 9–11, 13, 54
- and emotional intelligence 19
- and mental health issues 165
- and mindfulness 53
- non-judging 46
- and productivity 21
- and resilience 16–17
- self-compassion 109–110
- team coaching 107–111, 128–33
Compassion Focused Therapy (CFT) 9, 108, 141
competitiveness 98, 112
Confucius 54

Conscious Coaching xv–xvi, 3, 5–6
- and approach system 37
- body, mind and emotions 32
- building rapport 57–72
- coaching ourselves 41–3
- competencies 54–5
- and deep listening 61–3
- facilitating learning and results 74–101
- leaders 11–12
- mindset 44–54, 105
- and neuroplasticity 31
- organizational culture 135, 136–52
- and the past 155
constellations 89–91, 124–5
Cook-Greuter, Susanne 167
'corridor coaching' 4, 56
counselling 5
courage 53–4
Cranfield University 129–31
culture see organizational culture
culture-based coaching 83–4, 88, 127–8
Cutland, Nick 13

Dalai Lama 53
de Haan, Erik 22, 57
deep listening 61–3, 115–16
Dench, Tim 139–40
directive style 68–9
discrepancy-based monitor 35, 36
doing mode 35, 36, 50
Dream On 16–17
Drucker, Peter 166
Duffy, Mollie 33
Dweck, Carol 45

Ellison, Rachel 42
emotional intelligence (EQ) xiv,
    13, 17–19
emotions 31–4, 156–8
empathic curiosity 58
Esquivel, Antonio María 84
Estés, Clarissa 71
ethical codes 55, 170–71
Euroclear 139–40
European Mentoring and Coaching
    Council 54, 135, 170
'Evolutionary-Teal' 167
EXACT model 92–3, 118, 178, 179

facilitative style 67–8, 113
'Fall of Lucifer' (Esquivel) 84
feedback 96–7
FELT model 74–8, 128
Fosslien, Liz 33
'four-eyed' model 93, 118, 179
Frederickson, Barbara 34
Future Self exercise 85–6, 127
Future Team exercise 127

generosity 53
Germer, Christopher 172
Gestalt theory 49, 148
Gilbert, Maria 22
Gilbert, Paul 9, 108
goal setting
  – one-to-one coaching 91–3
  – team coaching 117–18
Goodwin, Janine 21–2
Grant, Anthony 14, 18, 28
gratitude 51–2, 71
Gregersen, Hal 125–6

Gregersen brainstorming process
    125–7
group coaching 4
GROW model 91–2, 117, 178, 179
growth mindset 45–6

'Halos and Horns' model
    94–7, 113
Hawkins, Peter 103–4, 118–19
Hellinger, Bert 89
Hutton, James 29

idealization 98, 112
impatience 47–8
Institute of Employment Studies
    (IES) 129–31
Institute of Leadership &
    Management 19, 28, 143
integrity 54
International Coach Federation
    (ICF) 3, 28, 54, 142, 171

Jonah's story 163–4
judgement 46, 94–7, 155

Kabat-Zinn, Jon 6, 7, 44
Karpman, Stephen 99
Kasozi, Anthony 22
Kegan, Robert 167
kindness 53
  – loving kindness meditation
    110–112
  – and mental health issues 165
  – self-compassion break
    109–110
Kline, Nancy 147–8

Laloux, Frederic 167, 168
Langer, Ellen 7
Lao Tzu 23
leadership
 – agile leadership 13, 22–7
 – coaching xv
 – Conscious Coaching 11–12
Legal & General 20
letting go/be/in 46–7, 78, 123
lifeline exercise 72–4
Lilley, Rachel 150–52
listening 61–3, 115–16
location coaching 80–82, 128

manager-as-coach 11–12
María's story 84
Maslow, Abraham 167
Megginson, David 135–6
Mental Health Foundation 7
mental health issues xi, 33, 159–65
 – see also stress
mentoring xiv, 5
military 129–31
mind
 – and body 31–4
 – modes 35–7
 – neuroplasticity 30–31
mindfulness xiii–xiv, xv–xvi, 3,
   6–8, 13, 44, 54
 – and agile leadership 23–7
 – art-based coaching 88
 – being mode 50, 51
 – belly breathing 164
 – and bias 94–6
 – building rapport 58–9
 – CID-CLEAR model 119–22

 – and compassion 10, 53
 – compassion-focused imagery
   exercise 108
 – Conscious Coaching culture
   137–8, 146–52
 – and courage 53
 – deep listening 61–3, 115–16
 – and emotional intelligence
   18–19
 – FELT model 74–8
 – 'four-eyed' model 93
 – Future Self exercise 85–6
 – generosity and kindness 53
 – Getting mindful practice 8
 – gratitude and appreciation 51–3
 – labelling emotions 157
 – letting go 47
 – lifeline exercise 72–4
 – location coaching 80–82
 – mini body scan 32–3
 – multiple perspectives 86–8,
   123–4
 – and neuroplasticity 31
 – non-judging 46
 – and patience 48
 – and productivity 21
 – and resilience 15–16
 – self-coaching 42–3
 – self-compassion break 109–110
 – SOAR practice 162–3
 – Systemic Constellations 89–91,
   124–5
 – teachers 41, 171–2
 – team coaching 128–33
 – thoughts 70–71
 – Triangle of Awareness 8–9

– and trust 47
– walking 79–80
Moorhead, Jon 29

National Institute for Health and
    Clinical Excellence (NICE) 6–7
nature 82
Neff, Kristin 109, 172
neuroplasticity 30–31
News UK 29
non-directive style 68–9
non-judging 46
non-striving 50–51
nourishing and depleting exercise
– one-to-one coaching 161
– team coaching 133–4
O'Connor, Sean 14, 28
one-to-one coaching
– building rapport 57–72
– Conscious Coaching mindset
    44–55
– ethical, legal and professional
    guidelines 55, 170–71
– facilitating learning and results
    74–101
– planning sessions 176–80
– programme planning 56, 173–5
organizational change 14, 27–9
organizational culture xv, 135, 155, 156
– coaching 135–6
– Conscious Coaching 136–52
Orriss, Miriam 99–100
Ozvision 71

parallel process 98–9, 112
paraphrasing 64, 116

patience 47–8
Pearl, David 83
Penman, Danny 32, 172
Pinsent Masons 146–9
prefrontal cortex (PFC) 31
presence 106
presenteeism xi, 50
productivity 13, 14, 19–22
projection 97–8, 112
PwC 4

questioning 64–8, 116
– Gregersen brainstorming
    process 125–7
Ramanathan, Ram 26–7
rapport
– one-to-one coaching 58–61
– team coaching 106
Ratcliff, John 16–17
reflecting 64, 116
reframing 69–70
relationship dynamics
– one-to-one coaching
    97–101, 155
– team coaching 112–13
Renolit 24
resilience xiv, 13, 14–17
– team coaching 128–9, 133–4
– tips for working on 160
Roffey Park 11
Runeckles, Matthew 26–7

Segal, Zindel 35
self-coaching 42–3
self-compassion 109–110
Semler, Richard 168

silence 67–8, 116
SOAR 162–3
Société Générale 26–7
Stanford University 141
storytelling 71–4, 127
Street Wisdom 83
stress xiv, 14, 159
 – breathing 164
 – tips for working on 160
striving 50–51
Suzuki, Shunryu 45
Systemic Constellations 89–91,
 124–5

Tagore, Rabindranath 51
team coaching 4, 102
 – issues to explore 103–112
 – moments 114
 – picking a coach 171
 – relationship dynamics 112–17
 – structuring interventions and
 designing actions 117–18
 – structuring sessions and meetings 118–34
therapy
 – and coaching 5
 – and compassion 10
 – and mindfulness 6–7

Thich Nhat Hanh 46, 62, 77
Thoreau, Henry David 79
Time to Think 147–8
Torbert, Bill 167
training 5, 141
Transactional Analysis (TA)
 98–100
Triangle of Awareness 8–9
trust 47, 58, 107
Turner, Eve 94, 160
Turner, Sophie 146–9

urban coaching 82–3

vulnerability 53–4

walking 79–88
Weick, Karl Edward 137
Welsh Government 149–52
West Midlands Employers
 Coaching and Mentoring Pool
 149
Whitmore, Sir John 91, 166
Williams, Mark 32, 172
Wilson, Carol 61, 92
Winner's Triangle 100–101

Zen Buddhism 6, 45

# PENGUIN PARTNERSHIPS

Penguin Partnerships is the Creative Sales and Promotions team at Penguin Random House. We have a long history of working with clients on a wide variety of briefs, specializing in brand promotions, bespoke publishing and retail exclusives, plus corporate, entertainment and media partnerships.

We can respond quickly to briefs and specialize in repurposing books and content for sales promotions, for use as incentives and retail exclusives as well as creating content for new books in collaboration with our partners as part of branded book relationships.

Equally if you'd simply like to buy a bulk quantity of one of our existing books at a special discount, we can help with that too. Our books can make excellent corporate or employee gifts.

Special editions, including personalized covers, excerpts of existing books or books with corporate logos can be created in large quantities for special needs.

We can work within your budget to deliver whatever you want, however you want it.

**For more information, please contact**
**salesenquiries@penguinrandomhouse.co.uk**